People of Alaska

ALASKA GEOGRAPHIC.

Volume 21, Number 3 / 1994

The Alaska Geographic Society

To teach many to better know and more wisely use our natural resources...

Editor
Penny Rennick

Production Director
Kathy Doogan

Staff Writer
L.J. Campbell

Circulation/Database Manager
Vickie Staples

Marketing Manager
Pattey Parker

Postmaster: Send address changes to
ALASKA GEOGRAPHIC®
P.O. Box 93370
Anchorage, Alaska 99509-3370

PRINTED IN U.S.A.

Board of Directors
Richard Carlson
Kathy Doogan
Penny Rennick

Robert A. Henning, *President Emeritus*

ISBN: 1-56661-022-2

Price to non-members this issue: $19.95

COVER: *Involved in the SEADOGS search and rescue program since 1989, Marianne McNair and her partner, Tiensing, patrol the steep, forested hillsides behind Juneau. (Pat Costello)*

PREVIOUS PAGE: *A fisherman mends a net on the dock at Kodiak. (Harry M. Walker)*

FACING PAGE: *The sea was home to the late Philip Campbell, who crewed aboard the old whaling ships that plied Alaska waters in the late 1800s. (Steve McCutcheon)*

ALASKA GEOGRAPHIC® is published quarterly by The Alaska Geographic Society, 639 West International Airport Road, Unit 38, Anchorage, AK 99518. Second-class postage paid at Anchorage, Alaska, and additional mailing offices. Copyright © 1994 by The Alaska Geographic Society. All rights reserved. Registered trademark: Alaska Geographic, ISSN 0361-1353; Key title Alaska Geographic.

THE ALASKA GEOGRAPHIC SOCIETY is a non-profit, educational organization dedicated to improving geographic understanding of Alaska and the North, putting geography back in the classroom and exploring new methods of teaching and learning.

SOCIETY MEMBERS receive *ALASKA GEOGRAPHIC*®, a quality publication that devotes each quarterly issue to monographic in-depth coverage of a northern geographic region or resource-oriented subject.

MEMBERSHIP in The Alaska Geographic Society costs $39 per year, $49 to non-U.S. addresses. ($31.20 of the membership fee is for a one-year subscription to *ALASKA GEOGRAPHIC*®.) Order from The Alaska Geographic Society, Box 93370, Anchorage, AK 99509-3370; phone (907) 562-0164, fax (907) 562-0479.

SUBMITTING PHOTOGRAPHS: Please write for a list of upcoming topics or other specific photo needs and a copy of our editorial guidelines. We cannot be responsible for unsolicited submissions. Submissions not accompanied by sufficient postage for return by certified mail will be returned by regular mail.

CHANGE OF ADDRESS: The post office does not automatically forward *ALASKA GEOGRAPHIC*® when you move. To ensure continuous service, please notify us six weeks before moving. Send your new address and your membership number or a mailing label from a recent issue of *ALASKA GEOGRAPHIC*® to: The Alaska Geographic Society, Box 93370, Anchorage, AK 99509-3370.

Color Separations:
GRAPHIC CHROMATICS
Printed by:
THE HART PRESS

ABOUT THIS ISSUE: It seems the most appropriate people to acknowledge for this issue are the people of Alaska themselves. But there are those who have worked especially hard to record Alaska's history through its citizens and we'd like to acknowledge their efforts. We thank Bruce Merrell and Dan Fleming, long-time keepers of the Alaska Collection at the Z.J. Loussac Library in Anchorage; Diane Brenner and Mina Jacobs, custodians of the archives at the Anchorage Museum; long-time Alaskans Steve McCutcheon and William Wakeland, whose photos have done more than most to record the changing lifestyle of Alaska and its people; Frank Norris of the National Park Service in Anchorage, who suggested names of those who deserved to have their stories told; and Ms. Gertrude Nelson Felzien, Ms. Elsie E. Hill, Mrs. Lilian Rivers Stolt and Betty Lou Broderick, who diligently researched the names of the ladies shown in the fashion show photo.

The Library of Congress has cataloged this serial publication as follows:

Alaska Geographic. v.1-
[Anchorage, Alaska Geographic Society] 1972-
v. ill. (part col.). 23 x 31 cm.
Quarterly
Official publication of The Alaska Geographic Society.
Key title: Alaska geographic, ISSN 0361-1353.

1. Alaska—Description and travel—1959-
—Periodicals. I. Alaska Geographic Society.

F901.A266   917.98'04'505   72-92087

Library of Congress   75[79112] MARC-S

Contents

Just Passing Through

In a sense we're all just passing through, a phenomenon more noticeable to the founder and long-time former editor of The Alaska Geographic Society who has spent decades in Alaska, than to those of us who have come in later years. But as that founder, Bob Henning, also says, some stay a little longer than others before passing on. This issue is about those who have stayed longer than most and who have made Alaska their home. Publicity has seldom visited most of these people; they are not household names except to those who know them directly. For the most part they are ordinary folks who have made a life in Alaska, accepting the challenges and the rewards of the North. Many, many more names could be added to this account of Alaska's people, and future issues will include profiles of some of them, but this issue is a beginning…a starting point in telling our readers about some of the fascinating folks who inhabit the Great Land.

The Beginning

When Vitus Bering first anchored a Russian sailing ship off Alaska's shores in July 1741, his arrival marked the beginning of waves of western cultures that would challenge and eventually overwhelm the territory's Native cultures. True, most of Alaska's Natives went about their daily lives for decades, with only the Aleuts of the Aleutian Islands feeling the direct effects of an invading lifestyle, but in time the white culture spread throughout Native Alaska. Today modern conveniences and the latest in electronic gadgets are as much a part of rural Native communities as they are of Anchorage and Fairbanks. Yet, some Native elders still recall their parents telling about the arrival of the first whites into their homeland.

By the 18th century, Alaska's Natives had developed wide cultural differences. Invading Westerners, most of whom were unfamiliar with these differences, designated Alaska's Natives as Eskimos in the north and west, Indians in the Interior, Aleuts in the Aleutians, a jumble of Indians and Eskimos along the southcentral coast, and Indians in the southeastern panhandle. A subsistence lifestyle was common to all. Intermittent trading and shipwrecks brought them pots of copper, knives of metal and other hints that different cultures lay beyond their shores. It is unclear how the social structure of early prehistoric people operated, but by the time Westerners were exploring North America, some of Alaska's Native people had developed a cultural hierarchy of rulers and ruled. Those who could call up the spirits, heal the sick, lead in battle and provide well for their families became the rulers; those who couldn't became the ruled.

After 1741, the Russian culture, slowly at first and then more quickly, permeated the Aleutian Islands and coastal areas of the mainland. Following the initial wave of explorers came fur hunters and traders, in many cases an unruly lot whose excesses prompted the Russian rulers to grant a monopoly to the Russian

Angela and Joe Odinzoff add to their winter food supply while ice fishing at Stebbins on the south shore of Norton Sound. (James M. Simmen)

American Co., which they charged in part with bringing order to the colony. Churchmen followed, encouraged by visions of an orderly society and Natives just waiting to be enlightened.

One aspect of this order was to count the inhabitants of Russian America. Logistics and politics prevented Russian census-takers from reaching many residents of the North American colony and, in any event, Russians were inclined to only count those Natives directly under their control, mostly those along the coasts and in a few interior river valleys. Counts vary as to the number of people in Alaska in 1867 when Russian America became United States territory. Fifty thousand has been the number commonly tossed about but many accounts indicate that this number is exaggerated.

Not until 1880 did the United States make its first territory-wide effort to count Alaskans. Relying largely on reports from Special Agent Ivan Petroff, the census-takers tallied 33,426 residents, substantially below the 50,000 claimed for Russian America. In the Arctic, Capt. E.E. Smith of the revenue cutter *Thomas Corwin* counted 3,094 residents — no whites and one Native for every 40 and one-half square miles — for the entire 125,245-square-mile Arctic Division. Captain Smith's count covered the northwestern and western sections of the Seward Peninsula and all lands north of the Yukon River watershed.

The early censuses were a bit imprecise, and it seems that census district boundaries were just as flexible as were the counts. By 1890, the Arctic Division, for instance, had stretched to include all of the Seward Peninsula, St. Lawrence Island and the lands north of the Yukon basin. And where there had been no whites residing in the division 10 years earlier, there were now 391, but still no white females.

The final tally for the 1890 census places 32,052 people living in Alaska. These figures also reflect the growing diversification of nationalities living in the territory. Hawaiians, Malays and Portugese mulattos from the Cape Verde Islands, most of whom were involved in the whaling industry, were just a few of the nationalities census-takers noted in Alaska.

The returns for 1890 were published as a separate report on the population and resources of Alaska. In his letter of transmittal, the Superintendent of the Census comments briefly on the difficulties encountered by the census enumerators in Alaska:

This remote portion of our territory presents difficulties in the way of enumeration scarcely conceivable in the older portion of the country. On an estimated area greater than that of all the states north of Tennessee and east of the Mississippi there is a population less than in most single counties of the populous east.

Alaska's population took a big jump at the turn of the century, mostly as a result of the large influx of prospectors, miners and get-rich-quick artists involved in the gold rush. Census-takers in 1900 counted 63,592 people within the 590,884 square miles then calculated as the size of Alaska. These numbers credited Alaska's population with one-tenth of one person per square mile

Subsequent censuses reflect slow, steady growth with one exception: the decline to 55,036 in 1920 from the 64,356 of 1910. The population takes another big jump from 1930 to 1940, reaching 72,524 as of Oct. 1, 1939. For the 1930 and 1940 censuses, the counts

FACING PAGE: *Anchorage was just 12 years old when the town's ladies gathered at the Empress Theater for a show featuring fashions for women from the time of Eve until 1927. From left are: Rose Rivers Holdiman, Emily Ryberg, LuLu Roop Bowden, unidentified, Billie Nottveit, Ruth Holdiman Smith, Gertrude Mulcahy, Velma Kvale, Decema Kimball Andresen, Vida Deigh Lee, Ester Nelson Laughlin, Enid Marsh, Gertrude Nelson Felzien, Doris (Doady) Lawson Ervin Walkowski, Betty Watson, Eva Allenbaugh MacDonald, Harriett LaZelle and Lilian Rivers Stolt. (Courtesy of Pattey Parker)*

ABOVE: *The New Archangel Dancers symbolize a time when Alaska was Russian territory and the Imperial rulers had their colonial capital at Sitka. The dancers perform at Centennial Hall in downtown Sitka. (Harry M. Walker)*

were actually taken on Oct. 1 of the previous year because of the climate and the difficulty of reaching people dispersed over such a wide area. The 1950 census noted another big increase to 128,643, and each census since has recorded a substantial increase. By 1990, Alaska's population had reached 550,043.

This number continues to fluctuate with the cyclical nature of the state's economy. But even with the boom-and-bust mentality, those who have stayed to make Alaska their home have outnumbered those who have left.

Marco Polo referred to the northwestern corner of what is now North America as the "Region of Darkness." Perhaps, but early people managed to adapt quite well and to develop a sophisticated civilization. Westerners who arrived after 1741 may be more likely to think of the territory as the Region of Opportunity.

—*Penny Rennick*

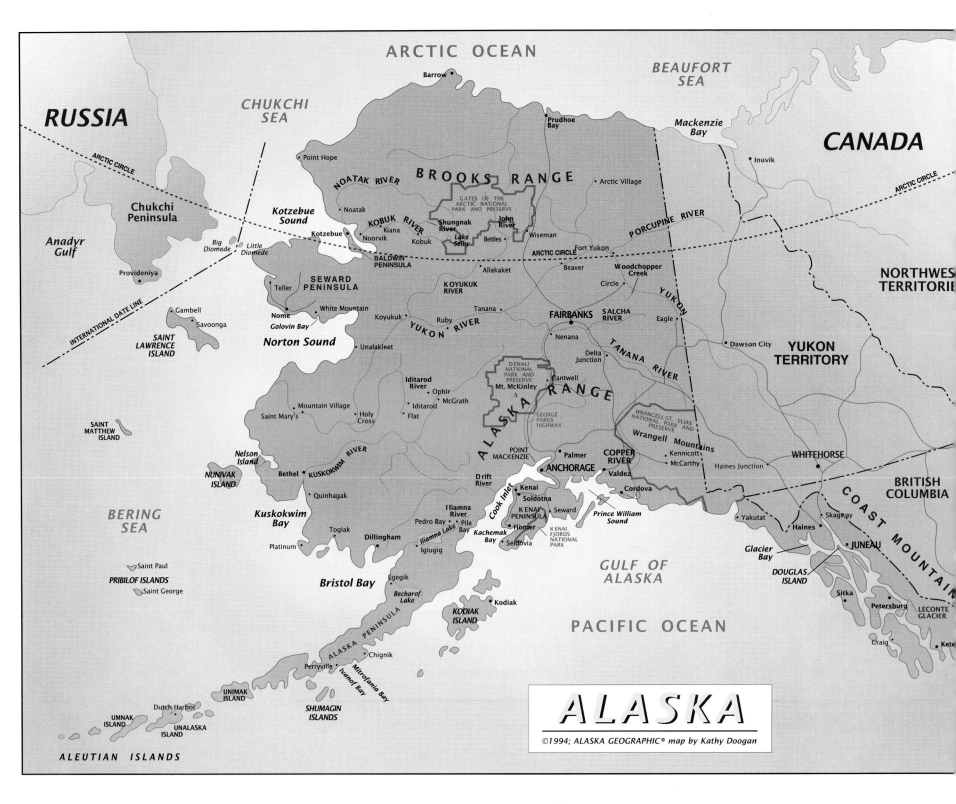

Bill Schneider
Conservator of Alaska's Stories

By Roger Kaye

Editor's note: *Roger, of Fairbanks, is a pilot and free-lance writer.*

In a small apartment for the elderly in downtown Fairbanks, distant memories of a frail and deeply wrinkled Eskimo woman, some stretching as far back as the end of nomadic times, are being recounted and preserved.

Oral historian Bill Schneider is a rapt listener. His subject, Tishu Ulen, is the last living link with the turn-of-the-century era of the Upper Koyukuk country. Unmindful now of his tape recorder, she has forgotten this is an interview and is enjoying his interest in her life. With the subtle guidance, never direction, of his questions, she begins with stories of her parents, of their wanderings along the arctic coast and through the Brooks Range; of how they nearly starved when the caribou couldn't be found; of how her family settled into the gold camp of Wiseman and of her baptism by traveling missionary Hudson Stuck.

Schneider's approving nods and appreciative smiles bring out the details of her 350-mile, dog-team-and-raft journey to Kotzebue in 1914. Later, her hands move as if they grasp for toboggan handles as she relives, more as reality than recollection, the cold evening her dog team began breaking through the ice at Big Lake, east of Wiseman in the Brooks Range.

After 35 minutes Schneider notices that Ulen is tiring; she's not been well lately. He turns off the tape recorder, thanks her and asks if he could come again. He says he would especially like to record more stories of her early childhood and settling into Wiseman.

Ulen smiles, "You can come 'round anytime I'm feelin' OK."

Before the next interview, the wealth of experiences Ulen had yet to share were lost. Forever. For such reasons, Bill Schneider is a man racing against time.

Recently, in his office in the Alaska and Polar Regions Archives at the University of Alaska Fairbanks, Schneider talked about his calling and that evening with Ulen three years ago. Hair ruffled, given to wearing sandals, worn green jeans and a wool shirt with holes at the elbows, appearances belie the 46-year-old professor's position, but words reveal his enchantment.

"Oral histories are my touchstones with places," he said. "Life stories in their original words conjure up images that enrich those of us who wonder . . . what was it actually like to be there in the past? It's terribly seductive."

Schneider has done nearly 500 recordings of Alaska Natives, politicians and pioneers. Some of his subjects were prominent, but most were ordinary people who led ordinary lives; his is grassroots history that provides personal and intimate context for the past.

The Ulen tape, he said, contributes to the historic record of the Koyukuk region, but more importantly, it breathes freshness into its history. "Tishu's vivid

Bill Schneider, his wife, Sidney, and daughter, Willa, launch their raft onto the Koyukuk River at Bettles. The Schneider family was floating the Koyukuk, through the heart of the northern Interior, homeland of the late Tishu Ulen whom Schneider had interviewed for his oral history project. (Darlene Masiak, courtesy of Bill Schneider)

accounts enable us to catapult back in time, to be there when the events she describes took place."

That happened last summer on one of Schneider's wilderness trips with his wife and 5-year-old daughter. Floating down the Koyukuk River they saw wildlife and scenery, but only traces of the area's rich history. "Most tangible evidence of those times was gone," he lamented, "but Tishu's accounts kept coming back to me." They offered a different time perspective, he said,

another way to know the area.

That the public could not similarly enjoy the university's vast collection of historic treasures has long frustrated Schneider. So four years ago he pioneered what is now considered one of the most innovative means of preserving and sharing personal histories: Project Jukebox. Jukebox is a multimedia computer system that brings together the collected recordings, photographs and transcripts relating to archived subjects and makes them accessible. It's

interactive and user friendly, Schneider emphasized. With the push of a button, anyone can view the biography, photos and maps related to someone, say, Tishu Ulen, while listening to her tape. "This technology lets us liberate the archives," Schneider said. "It comes closer to providing a sense of who these people are and the essence of what they've shared than we've ever been able to get before."

Before he became a family man just seven years ago, Schneider was, in most respects, the stereotypical ivory-tower scholar, singularly absorbed in his research and teaching, constantly writing papers, articles and books on Alaska history and anthropology. His childhood education at an East Coast "coat-and-tie" academy had prepared him well for academic achievements, but he missed much.

"I never learned how to fix a car," he admitted, "and never had the time to take in popular culture."

"It's fun to tease him about that," says his wife, Sidney. "He doesn't know TV personalities, doesn't even know who Mick Jagger is." [Mick Jagger is the lead singer of the music group Rolling Stones, who achieved worldwide fame, beginning in the 1960s.]

Project Jukebox

Professor Bill Schneider is passionate about the history of Alaska's people. His Project Jukebox is an outgrowth of that passion.

Project Jukebox involves recordings of oral histories gathered by Schneider, which are digitized for an interactive computer display and matched with photos and text relating to the oral history. Schneider says each project costs about $50,000, and the National Park Service, various Native organizations, the North Slope Borough and the Pioneers of Alaska, among others, have hired him to do interviews and prepare the histories.

There are Project Jukebox outlets around the state, mostly located at the headquarters of various national parks, or in the central communities for individual projects, such as Tanana for a project on the middle Yukon River area. The original tapes remain at the Rasmuson Library at the University of Alaska Fairbanks.

Schneider, curator of oral histories for the library, has also established an intern program where Alaskans from the Bush come to Fairbanks and are trained in indexing and digitizing oral histories. The interns select recordings and return with them to their home communities. There they index and digitize the histories, at the same time enabling others in the community to see the value of oral histories and to learn more about their own culture. Once the tapes are digitized, they can be retrieved and scanned by key word on the Rasmuson Library's computers, making the information on the tapes more accessible to the general public.

"But he's become a great family man," she says, noting that he enjoys his equal role in raising their daughter, Willa. Vacations and most weekends are family times, often for camping, canoeing or mushing their six huskies.

"My family taught me a greater fullness in life," said Schneider.

Sidney agrees, but "he's still driven and consumed by his work. Outside his work and family, there's little room for other things in his life."

Schneider found his career in college, although he suspects his affinity for different lifeways came from his mother, a social worker. He began a graduate program in anthropology at Bryn Mawr in Pennsylvania, and did his first fieldwork in the Canadian Arctic at Rankin Inlet.

While staying with an Inuit family, the markedly sensitive student encountered his first doubt about anthropological research. "I began to wonder, 'What am I doing out here poking into these peoples'

Bill Schneider talks with Moses Cruikshank, an Athabaskan, about his life in the Interior. The project resulted in the book The Life I've Been Living *(1986). Cruikshank was born on the Black River near Fort Yukon in 1906. Raised at the mission at Nenana, he mushed dogs for the missionaries when they made their winter rounds to the villages, helped build the Alaska Railroad, and later was a gold prospector, hunter and trapper. (Rik Van Stone, University of Alaska Press)*

business?" A few years later, while beginning his Ph.D. dissertation on the Yukon River village of Beaver, the villagers made it poignantly clear that they did not wish "to be put under a microscope" as theoretical case studies are wont to do.

"I struggled with that concern," Schneider said, "and it led to a turning point in my career." He refocused his dissertation, seeking an understanding of the culture through life histories of the residents. His approach proved less intrusive, and resulted in a publication they could value.

In the introduction to his dissertation, Schneider explained how preserving life histories can help Natives in their effort to re-establish their sense of ethnic identity. "Even though they may not at present be turning to the old people, they will someday," he predicted, "and if the old people are gone, then they will need the record of what the old people have said about their history and culture."

But Schneider's face stiffens with protest at the suggestion that altruism is his foremost motivation. "No, I do this because I find tremendous pleasure in being around the people I work with. The stories they share enrich my life," he said. "The enjoyment is mostly mine."

Yet among the most rewarding images inhabiting the anthropologist's fervent imagination, there is an anonymous face. It belongs to some elder's yet-unborn descendant, and Schneider's mind's eye visions it glowing as "he discovers my work and says, 'Gol, this is a gold mine.'" ■

James Mumigana Nageak, Leona Kisautaq Okakok and Bill Schneider look over material from the book Kusiq *(1991), the recountings from an oral history by Waldo Bodfish Sr. of Eskimo life along the arctic coast. Nageak and Okakok collaborated with Schneider, providing background and understanding of Eskimo culture and translating and interpreting Bodfish's Eskimo language for Schneider. (Richard Veazey, Rasmuson Library)*

Fishermen clean their red salmon subsistence catch at King Salmon on the Alaska Peninsula. Southwestern Alaska supports the world's largest red salmon runs. (James M. Simmen)

Loy Green

By Bill Sherwonit

Editor's note: *An Anchorage resident, Bill is a well-known free-lance writer and the author of two books.*

On a beautiful July day in the Wrangell Mountains, Loy Green sits in his McCarthy cabin and reminisces about the town's "good old days" as he remembers them, and laments its present state of being.

The byproduct of an early 1900s copper-mining operation at nearby Kennicott, McCarthy sits deep within one of America's most spectacular wildernesses. On its doorstep are rugged peaks and glacier-fed rivers.

For decades the town served as the quintessential haven for reclusive Alaskans seeking a quiet, simple backcountry lifestyle. "It was perfect for a hermit like me," Green says smiling.

But now McCarthy has been transformed into a tourist town. And there's no going back, because this small — only 20 to 30 people live here year-round — end-of-the-road community has been tagged the principal gateway into the nation's largest park unit, 13.2-million-acre Wrangell-St. Elias National Park and Preserve. And Wrangell-St. Elias, a mountain wilderness the size of six Yellowstones, has been discovered by the masses.

This bothers Green, who at 65 is one of the town's oldest residents, whether judged by age or length of stay. Past curator of the McCarthy-Kennicott Historical Museum, his passions run to music, painting and philosophizing.

Green settled here in 1967, lured by McCarthy's ties to mining. "I'm not a miner myself, but I've always been attracted to miners and the mining atmosphere; you know, I was raised in a farming community but my dad worked at a mine in Colorado not unlike Kennicott."

During its heyday in the early 1900s, perhaps 100 to 150 people lived in McCarthy. But the bawdy town lost most of its residents, and its wildness, when the Kennicott mine and the Copper River & Northwestern Railroad closed in 1938. Only a few people stayed on, to scratch out a subsistence lifestyle.

Still, interest in the area's mineral deposits didn't completely fade away. When Green arrived, geologists were still combing the area for additional copper deposits; he hired on with an exploration crew and worked as camp cook for the next five summers. He also spent three years at Kennicott's deserted mining complex, acting as a caretaker.

"A lot of people still believed there were more riches out there, waiting to be discovered," he says. "This is still supposed to be one of the highest mineralized areas in the country." But no new mother lodes were ever found.

Back in the late 1960s, only four others called McCarthy home. And no businesses catered to outsiders. Even the McCarthy Lodge had temporarily shut down. "If you'd dropped into McCarthy then, you'd have found a peaceful, quiet community, a really good life," Green recalls. "But now...I'm alarmed and disappointed by what's happening. The most disheartening thing is the changed attitudes since tourism entered the picture. Hard-core competition is happening big-time and I won't support it. We need to develop a win-win philosophy."

McCarthy's residents got a glimpse of the town's tourism future in 1975, when a new bridge built across the Kennicott River opened McCarthy to vehicle traffic. Currently residents and visitors must cross via a hand-pulled tram.

"There was a ribbon cutting and everything," Green says. "Then in come the cars, a line of them with dust rolling up. It was like 'Wow, we're in McCarthy.' The real McCarthy disappeared right then; it could have been any roadside stop. I saw and experienced it. And I didn't like what I saw."

The bridge lasted only one season, getting washed away the following spring. So Loy and his neighbors got their community back. But deep down, he knew it was only a matter of time before McCarthy disappeared for good.

Not until the early 1990s did McCarthy have what might be called a business district. Today the town boasts a lodge, hotel, bed and breakfast, pizza parlor, espresso bar, two air taxi operators, two shuttle-bus services and a backcountry guide outfitter, all a reflection of the tourist boom.

Green, a self-described maverick, isn't much interested in the "general tourist," though he once made a foray into the visitor industry. Back in the mid-1980s, he helped establish the McCarthy-Kennicott Museum and for six years,

using a back room as his own living quarters, he worked as museum curator. He also used some of the building's space as his painting gallery .

At first, no more than a dozen or so people visited the museum. But as their numbers increased, Green realized he wasn't the best person for the job. "I felt trapped in my own room," he says. "So I moved out."

While doing his best to cope with McCarthy's newest incarnation as a tourist town, Green offers his own vision for the town.

"If tourism is here to stay, which it

Loy Green plays his trumpet during McCarthy's Independence Day parade. A fancier of the arts, Loy would like to see McCarthy, the tiny community at the end of the McCarthy Road in Wrangell-St. Elias National Park and Preserve, become an artists' colony rather than a tourist trap. (Bill Sherwonit)

seems to be," he says, "then how can we create an atmosphere that would attract musicians, artists, sculptors, painters? An artists' colony. That's what I would like to see." ∎

Charlie Kelly

By Bob King

Editor's note: *A resident of Dillingham, Bob is a free-lance writer and broadcaster for public radio station KDLF.*

Charlie Kelly lives a subsistence life. He also runs a fishing boat in one of Alaska's most aggressive fisheries, serves on the village council and the board of the regional health corporation. Times are changing in rural Alaska, but if you ask Charlie Kelly what he does he will tell you he simply lives a subsistence life.

"A lot of people come up and ask 'what do you do all winter'? Well, keeping a household in the village and making it comfortable is a lot of work. Me and my wife are busy trying to put up the last of our fish. I just threw the net in this morning. I got ducks to hunt and berries to put away. It's not just sitting at home."

Charlie Kelly was born in 1949 in Egegik, a small village that surrounds two canneries in lower Bristol Bay. The run of sockeye salmon to nearby Becharof Lake has been exceptionally productive in recent years, producing a record catch of more than 20 million sockeye in 1993. That catch also attracted a record fleet of more than 1,000 gillnetters, and the feeding frenzy of the fleet as they jockey for position along the north line has made Egegik infamous in recent years.

"You'd never believe it until you see it. The boats are bigger and wider with more horsepower, and if you're in their way

Charlie Kelly has lived in both the Native and white worlds in Alaska. Born in Egegik on Bristol Bay, he graduated from high school in Anchorage, had a good job during the boom years of construction of the trans-Alaska pipeline, but opted to give his job up in favor of returning to Egegik, where he could be his own boss. As with many residents of western Alaska, Charlie supplements his commercial fishing income with subsistence hunting, trapping and fishing. (Mark Dolan)

they'll just move you aside. If you have a wood boat they'll just crumble you if they hit you just right. I have a big fiberglass boat but the boats that are coming up now are aluminum, have 600, 700 horsepower. They're geared up just to catch fish and if you're in front of them, they'll move you aside. It's everyone for themselves out there."

It wasn't always that way. Charlie remembers that Egegik was a gentlemanly fishery when he started fishing in his early teens. But a lot of things have changed in Egegik since then. Health care has changed dramatically. Egegik now has two village health aides. Charlie recalls when Egegik residents depended on the village healer, a woman named Virginia Albert.

"She had quill treatments, she would bleed you if you had muscle pains or back pains. She liked to use her little knives and needles and herbs. I remember when I was a little kid I had impetigo real bad and she cleared it up. She used some kind of moss and dirt and just packed it. It was pretty effective."

Like a lot of rural families, Charlie's parents moved from the village to give their children a better education. After graduating from Dimond High School in Anchorage, Charlie stayed in town. It was the early pipeline days and jobs were easy to come by. One day, however, he gave it all up.

"I was working eight-to-five and getting Saturday and Sunday off. I had a really good job setting up trailers. I worked and worked and worked. One morning I just got tired of it. Told the wife to quit her job. She had a good job with Union Oil. It was a February morning. We chartered an Otter, packed our gear and came down."

They brought their aspirations back with them to Egegik as well. Both Charlie and his wife, Shirley, went to work on the village council and helped build safe water and sewer systems, a new fire hall, recreation center and clinic. Egegik is now working on a new airport and dock. And Egegik will need to continue to grow in the years ahead. Like many rural communities, Egegik is experiencing a baby boom. A third of its population is now children, Charlie estimates, putting an increased demand on all village services.

But despite all the changes in village life and commercial fishing, Charlie Kelly still essentially lives a lifestyle unchanged from that of his parents and their parents.

"I'll get my caribou and fish together. I salt fish, freeze fish, get all my caribou put away. I'm waiting for winter to start so I can go ice fishing, hunting and trapping. There's plenty of fur out here. Beaver, land otter, wolverine and fox. The price isn't right but it keeps you busy.

"Yeah, I enjoy my subsistence style of life. It's been good to me. It's been good to my parents. And there's no other job that I'd rather have than be a commercial fisherman. Being my own boss. With commercial fishing and gathering what we can in the fall and winter, we're set. If you make enough to buy your oil, your flour and sugar and 20 pounds of coffee, you're set for the winter." ■

Contestants in the Barefoot Race at the Cantwell Rhondy sprint for the finish line. (Michael R. Speaks)

Carl Anderson

By Charles P. Wohlforth

Editor's note: *Charles is a free-lance writer living in Anchorage.*

Each morning of his childhood, Carl Anderson woke surrounded by water and tidal mud on the dock his father built on the waterfront of Anchorage. Salt water already ran in his veins. His grandfather, Jack Anderson, had come from Norway on a square-rigged ship, rounding Cape Horn as a cabin boy before ending up in Seattle at age 13. By the time Carl was 13, he'd already been working on the water two years.

At 17, Anderson got his master's license. Although he was too young to be a ship's master, local Coast Guard officials winked at the rules—he already had more sea time than a lot of sailors twice his age—and Carl started operating a tugboat on the city's waterfront. His brother Andy started a company in Seward working the barge trade.

"I get seasick, so I decided I'd better stay in port, in the calm water," Carl explains.

That was 1974. This morning, 20 years later, Anderson wakes early at his home on Government Hill, a few hundred yards above the dock his father, also called Jack, built. A 710-foot container ship, the *Sealand Anchorage*, is approaching across Cook Inlet. From the bluff above the port, the summer sun brightens the water like liquid electricity. Anderson jumps in his Dodge pickup and drives to the dockside, where the tugboat *Stellar Wind* is waiting.

Almost 90 percent of the cargo entering Alaska comes across this dock. Almost everything Alaskans eat, wear, live in, drive, or read arrives on the ships owned by Sealand and Totem Ocean Trailer Express (TOTE) that call on Anchorage on Sundays and Tuesdays each week. With modern low-inventory retailing techniques, those ships form the state's lifeline; if they stopped running, store shelves would quickly empty. And every ship needs Anderson. He owns and operates the tugboats that dock almost every ship that comes to the port.

In the wheelhouse, Anderson noshes a buttered Pop Tart while he listens for the captain of the *Sealand Anchorage* on the radio. A young crewman in a black Pittsburgh Pirates baseball cap runs a tattered American flag up a halyard.

The 85-foot *Stellar Wind* is a hard-working boat, but she still looks as clean and trim as she did a year ago, when she came out of the Tristar Marine shipyard

FACING PAGE: This 1966 view shows Anderson Dock at the Port of Anchorage from Brown's Point on Government Hill. The Anderson family lived in an apartment on the second floor above the seaward end of the building. In these years the family operated the tugs Arctic Wind, Fair Wind *and* South Wind. Crowley *vessels are tied up at the end of the dock on this summer day, while* Foss' Alaska Husky *is at the end of the dock on the right. (Courtesy of Carl Anderson)*

in Ballard, Wash. Built to Anderson's exact specifications, she is uniquely suited for conditions in Anchorage: heavy ice, currents that run up to 7 knots, and huge ships that can get in trouble when wind, current or mechanical failure go against them.

Anderson climbs down two decks, below the galley and crews' quarters, to the engine room. The twin 1,500- horsepower engines are not unusual for a tug of this type, but the propulsion system is. Below a huge, round case of gears, the *Stellar Wind*'s two props each can pivot in a complete 360-degree circle.

The vessel has no rudder, but it can spin around like a top, stop on a dime, push a ship sideways and go backwards as fast as it goes forward.

"The horsepower is the same, but you can do so much more with it," he says. "I can put that horsepower in any direction I want."

He starts the engines and the boat roars. The *Sealand Anchorage* is nearing the port. With lines thrown off, Anderson drops the engines in gear and races away from the dock. He has no steering wheel. Instead, he sits with his two hands on two joysticks that control each engine's speed and direction. The *Stellar Wind* bolts nimbly across the water to intercept the 20,965-ton ship capable of carrying some 700 highway trailers.

More than 50 years ago, when Anderson's father and grandfather arrived in Alaska, almost everything about the waterfront and commerce in Anchorage was different. The city was a small town, with about 3,000 population, and not an important one; it had only 5 percent of the state's population, compared with 40 percent today. The Andersons went into business in the 1930s linking Anchorage to the other coastal towns, running mail, passengers and cargo between Anchorage, Seward and Seldovia.

World War II wiped out their business, as the military confiscated the Anderson's vessels, over the objections of the U.S. Postal Service. But when the building boom of the post-war years began, the Andersons got in the tug and barge business. Jack Anderson had contracts delivering construction materials for Cold War defense projects and, as oil developed in Cook Inlet the late 1950s and early '60s, he carried that equipment, too.

"He had a dozen tugs by then," Anderson says. "Building platforms, carrying pipelines down there. And, of course, during all that time he was building Anderson Dock."

The dock was the second major cargo dock in Anchorage, after the so-called "Army Dock," which was destroyed by the 1964 earthquake.

"I lived on Anderson Dock all the way up to '70," Carl Anderson says. "First we started out in a 70-foot trailer house, and then after the earthquake Dad built a warehouse with a three-bedroom apartment. So when you woke up in the morning you were surrounded by water, and you could see everything. We had bikes and we could pretty much have free rein. I've lived within sight of the mud flats all my life."

Carl began his life of working on the water at age 11, helping paint the legs of a Drift River oil platform. At age 12 he towed logs in Jakolof Bay, a branch of Kachemak Bay. He crossed the Gulf of Alaska. Then, in 1970, Jack Anderson sold the dock. Carl moved to Government Hill and in 1974 started docking ships in Anchorage with a tugboat he built with his father and brother.

Today he is raising three children, ages 8, 10 and 13, with his wife, Debbie. For vacations they go boating on a 48-foot yacht in Washington's Puget Sound and San Juan Islands. Anderson leaves town only in the slow season, the cold months when ships will call out his relief skipper only two days a week. Few other boaters vacation in Puget Sound in winter, but Anderson says, "The kids don't know any different—they don't know it's cold down there."

Anderson looks his part. He is a wiry man with a prow of hair combed backwards from his high forehead. His speech is direct, with an accent that betrays a hint of his Norwegian heritage in a few of the old-fashioned colloquialisms he uses—phrases he probably learned as a child along with the ways of shipboard life. Even his house, looking over the bluff above the port, looks like it belongs to a ship's captain. There are Victorian details, a propeller in the yard, and an American flag flying on a pole.

The rounded bow of the *Stellar Wind*, padded with huge tractor tires, bumps against the wall-like hull of the *Sealand Anchorage*. Three Sealand crewmen take the end of a hawser from Anderson's crewman and fasten the tug to the ship. Anderson matches his speed, traveling diagonally through the water, to that of the huge ship as it plows ahead toward the dock. Shipping containers stacked four layers high tower above the tug.

"Everything you buy is right there in front of you," Anderson says, looking out the wheelhouse window in sparkling sunlight. "Campbell's soup, toilet paper, dresses. If you took these ships off line for 10 days, the grocery store shelves would disappear.

"Ninety-nine percent of the time, they don't need my help at all, but that one time out of 100, if anything goes wrong, it's millions of dollars. You can't touch anything with this stuff, even if you're going slow. It destroys stuff."

A freighter captain who miscalculated and hit the dock in 1978 caused $3 million in damage. Today, the Sealand ship nestles softly against the dock. It

The 85-foot Stellar Wind *displays the latest in tugboat design. The boat sports two 1,500-horsepower engines, and a propulsion system that allows the vessel to stop quickly, spin like a top and go backwards as fast as it goes forward. (Courtesy of Carl Anderson)*

appears Anderson's help won't be needed. Then the Sealand captain comes over the radio. A line is jammed and the *Anchorage* can't tie up. He asks Anderson to hold the ship against the dock so it won't drift in the current and hit one of the other two ships at the dock.

Anderson quickly unties and pulls back from the *Anchorage*, then nudges his bow midships and pushes the ship directly against the dock, pinning it in place. Prop wash roils out behind the unmoving tug. Now the Sealand crew has plenty of time to free their lines.

The voice of the Sealand captain comes over the radio again. How is Anderson's wife, Debbie? Does he have time to get

together for a chat sometime during the 16 hours the *Anchorage* will be in port? And what about the competing TOTE ship that is also tied up to the dock—when is it leaving?

"They've all been around for quite a while," Anderson says. "After 20 years you pretty much get to know everybody."

Communication isn't so easy with the foreign ships that occasionally call on Anchorage, bringing bulk materials like cement or carrying away logs or petroleum products to the Orient. Frequently, the ships will carry sailors and officers speaking three different languages. Living standards on the ships are sometimes far below what Americans

would expect—fish heads and rice, as Anderson says.

"The only people who know what's going on are me and the pilot," Anderson says. "You just have to get them up against the dock and hold them."

Now Sealand's lines are cleared and the *Stellar Wind* pulls away to head back to the dock. Eggs begin to fry in the galley. Anderson gets on his cellular telephone to work on a business deal.

Anderson has tried to expand his business. Five years ago, he built a barge dock at Point MacKenzie, a mile across Cook Inlet from Anchorage in the Matanuska-Susitna Borough. The borough built a road to the dock, but before much shipping could occur the biggest prospective customer collapsed — the state dairy farm project at Point MacKenzie.

Now borough officials are talking about building a port at the point to serve a planned iron ore reduction plant. If that happens, Anderson expects to be in good position with his barge dock. A U.S. Army Corps of Engineers project to dredge a shoal off Fire Island also may increase business in the Port of Anchorage by allowing larger ships to come in without having to synchronize their arrival and departure with the tides.

If those changes happen, they will be the first major changes in many years. "I've seen this port grow a lot in the last 20 years, but at the same time not a lot has changed," Anderson says. "The ships got bigger, but there's not any more of them."

For his part, the port's major tugboat operator doesn't expect to change, either. There isn't enough business to support competitors, and he remains popular and his service reliable.

"I've got kids in school for another 10 years, so I guess I'll be doing it for at least as long as that," he says.

And will they follow in his footsteps, as he did with his father, and his father before him? Anderson says it's too early to tell. But if he grew up with the sea in his veins, they are too. If he is the example, they will know their way around on boats.

As Anderson says, with honest pride, "There's not a lot of them out there in the world, but sometimes you find a real expert." ■

Ken and Hazel Heath put finishing touches on a batch of their "Alaska Wild Berry Products" in their home at Homer in fall 1948. Ken picked the berries, or the couple paid local children to pick for them. Hazel still lives in Homer, but has sold the business, which is thriving and is expanding to Anchorage. (William Wakeland)

Dick Proenneke first saw what was to become Lake Clark National Park in 1967. The next year he was back to begin construction on a cabin at Twin Lakes. Proenneke, 74, is still the only year-round resident of the Twin Lakes area, although summers see hikers stopping by on their treks through the area. Says Proenneke of his life in the wilderness: "How can you get lost if you don't care where you are?" (William Wakeland)

Be Sheldon

By Bill Sherwonit

Like so many people who've settled in Alaska, Bernice Sheldon, "Be" for short, first came north seeking adventure.

A 30-year-old Midwestern teacher who'd grown up on a Michigan farm, she and a couple of girl friends drove to Alaska in 1966, then spent several weeks roaming the state, both in their camper and by plane. Included in their itinerary were communities in Alaska's northwest and arctic regions: Nome, Kotzebue, Barrow.

"It was strictly a tourist thing at that point," she says.

Be (whose last name then was Schmidt) returned to America's heartland that fall. But she headed back north a year later, with different intentions. Adventure remained a primary goal. But this time, she planned to stay awhile. Find work. Settle into a niche.

"It was a time of life where I was in a transition mode," she says. "It was a good time to try something different."

Different indeed. Be's teaching experience landed her a job in Nome, with the region's head-start program. The position demanded that she travel to 13 villages, which made it all the more appealing.

While on one of her village trips, Be met an Inupiat Eskimo named Charlie Sheldon — a meeting that would drastically alter her life.

The son of nomadic reindeer herders, Sheldon had been born in the Brooks Range as his family traveled south from the North Slope to the Kobuk Valley. Like his parents, Charlie led a nomadic lifestyle. Besides herding reindeer, he spent much of his life hunting and trapping in the mountains and also mined for gold and jade along the Shungnak River.

Shortly after their meeting, "Charlie decided he wanted me as his wife, so he started to pursue me," Be recalls. "He wrote me lots of love letters. It was a very non-traditional courtship."

Even more unusual was their marriage.

Charlie Sheldon shows off some of his catch at Selby Lake in the western Brooks Range. (Be Sheldon)

Be Sheldon (right) has breakfast at the main lodge with a view west across Selby Lake through the window. (Courtesy of Be Sheldon)

Back in 1968, Be says, "It was pretty normal for a white male to marry a Native woman. But ours was the first marriage where an Eskimo man had married a white woman. It caused some difficulties. I was accepted by Charlie's best friends, but to most of the (Eskimo) community, I was always an outsider."

Their age difference proved less of a problem. Be was 31 when she married, while Charlie was 60. But a young-at-heart 60. "It was never an issue," she says.

The newlyweds spent their first year in Shungnak, an Eskimo village of about 200 people on the Kobuk River, then moved briefly to the even tinier community of Kobuk (population about 80), before returning "home" to Shungnak. There, Charlie continued to lead his subsistence lifestyle, while Be taught third and fourth grades at the local school.

Though never completely accepted into the community, Be learned to feel comfortable in Alaska's northwest.

"Charlie and I lived across (the river) from Shungnak, so we had long periods of solitude, where it was just the two of us," she says. "It was so nice to be in the midst of the wilderness, so exciting to go out on a snow machine and be in the midst of thousands and thousands of caribou, more animals than I'd ever imagined."

In summers, the Sheldons would move to the mountains, where Charlie had built a trap line cabin on Selby Lake, in the western Brooks Range.

Sheldon gained the rights to 80 acres of land during the 1970s, through the Alaska Native Claims Settlement Act, and the couple talked of constructing another, bigger cabin at Selby Lake. Maybe even start a wilderness lodge business.

Charlie died in 1979, not long after they'd "brushed out" a clearing for their proposed lodge. With her primary tie to the region now severed, Be moved to Cantwell, a small town along the Parks Highway, about 20 miles from Denali National Park. There she rejoined a couple of teacher friends she'd met in Shungnak.

But Be, who inherited Charlie's property, kept their Brooks Range dream alive. With help from friends, she finished the second cabin in the early 1980s. And in 1986, she opened her lodge — named Peace of Selby Wilderness — for business. A year later, she became business partners with Dee and Art Mortvedt, who'd also taught school at Shungnak.

Now 58, Sheldon is retired from teaching. But she's as busy as ever, it seems. Each winter for the past several years, she's traveled to Asia to do "mission work" in places like China, Korea and the Philippine Islands. And every summer, she returns to Peace of Selby, to help the Mortvedts run the lodge and reconnect with her Alaska roots.

"I have so many nice memories from there," she says. "It's a very special place." ∎

Charlie Sheldon and his wife, Be, pose in parkas during a visit to an Iowa classroom where they talked about their life in Alaska. (Courtesy of Be Sheldon)

Pete Abrams

By Bill Sherwonit

Born on Nelson Island in 1942, Yup'ik Eskimo Pete Abrams grew up in a community that was "isolated from everything." As a young boy, he remembers, there was no school. No sewer or running water. No telephones or even radio communication. No health-care facilities.

The nearest hospital or clinic was 150 miles away. Depending on the season, that meant three days' travel by boat, or two and one-half days by dog team.

A Catholic priest who occasionally visited the island helped the sick as best

A native of Nelson Island, in the Bering Sea off the coast of the Yukon-Kuskokwim delta, Pete Abrams carries on Yup'ik Eskimo traditions of his ancestors and at the same time operates a successful business and takes an active part in community affairs at Togiak, his home for about 30 years. (Mark Dolan)

Traditional games of skill among Alaska's Native people have become the focus of many competitions around the state. This youngster practices the Eskimo high kick at Russian Mission in the lower Kuskokwim River valley. (Harry M. Walker)

he could. And a government medical boat came by once a year, in the spring. But mostly, "when somebody got ill, the older people had their own remedies.... I remember seal oil, plants, human urine. And before I was born, magicians were used in healing. There were all kinds of stories, like how a certain magician would have his owns tools; a tiny bow here, a feather or something, or even a mouse....

"When I was small, there was a lot of sickness... it was a tough life, but we didn't mind it because that's how we were living. My forefathers were living like that too. They were survivors. We're all survivors, the Eskimos are."

Abrams was 15 when Nelson Island got its first school. Three years later he had to drop out; at 18, he was considered too old. Hungry for more formal education, he asked a teacher for guidance. Among the suggestions: join the Army.

So, in his late teens, Abrams exchanged Nelson Island's isolated, primitive world for California craziness. "Overnight, I went from dog teams and sailboats to escalators, TVs and traffic jams," he recalls. "It was two completely different worlds."

Abrams survived the culture shock and learned to bridge those two worlds; he's successfully adapted to western ways, while maintaining traditional Eskimo values and skills.

Now 52 and a resident of Togiak, where he settled about 30 years ago after meeting his future wife, Elsie, Abrams, like many rural Alaskans, is a jack of all trades: carpenter, plumber, electrician, commercial fishermen. He also runs a successful business and plays an active role in village politics, while maintaining subsistence connections with the land.

As a married man with seven children and a handful of grandchildren, Abrams sees the younger generations becoming ever more disconnected from their roots, a fact that saddens and worries him.

"My generation is separated between our world and the western world, about half and half," he says. "But our kids and their kids will have more knowledge of western culture than their own heritage.

"In the old days, our people knew how to survive on the ocean and on land. They were constantly observing everything, like animals do. Always paying attention. That's how the Eskimo was. But now we're spoiled. If we don't have running water, or the telephone isn't working, we're jumping up and down. We're not using our minds, arms and legs to survive."

It's Abrams' good fortune that his children and their children haven't lost interest in Eskimo traditions. All speak Yup'ik. And they ask "tons of questions" about how it used to be.

And so Pete Abrams passes along bits and pieces of his Yup'ik culture. He tells stories that were told to him, about the old ways, the magicians, the hardships, the celebrations and values. In sharing the stories, he is doubly blessed, because in their telling, he says, "My own memories are refreshed." ■

Edith Rose Bullock

By Robin Mackey Hill

Editor's note: *Robin Mackey Hill is a free-lance writer living in Anchorage. Robin interviewed Mrs. Bullock in 1993; Mrs. Bullock died May 8, 1994.*

Frail and stooped, Edith Bullock slowly crosses her living room floor and gingerly lowers herself into an armchair. Over her left shoulder, above the mantle, is a portrait of a village priest by Alaska artist Muriel Hannah. Over her right shoulder, above the bookcase carefully filled with books and periodicals on Alaska, is a small oil painting by Alaskan Fred Machetanz. A lone kayaker, his back to the painter, slowly paddles his skin boat between ice floes on his way, perhaps, to hunt seal. For Bullock, the painting provides welcome passage back to her days as owner of Kotzebue's B & R Tug and Barge and of time spent on the Seward and Baldwin peninsulas of northwestern Alaska.

From windows that stretch the length of her 10th floor, art-filled condominium. Bullock can look across all of downtown Anchorage. It's a view she enjoys. From the balcony, if one cranes far enough to the left, one can steal a glimpse of Cook Inlet and its mud flats. After living for two decades with expansive Kotzebue Sound as her backdrop, Bullock has no interest in craning her neck.

Settled in her seat, Bullock greets her guest. Then, prompted by a single question, she begins to tell again the story of her more than 50 years in Alaska, years spent as a placer miner, pioneering businesswoman, civic leader and territorial lawmaker. "This is my life," says Bullock, who was born Edith Rose in Red Lodge, Mont. "I can't imagine living anywhere else. My life before Alaska, I never think about it. It's like it never happened."

For Edith McVay, an only child raised by her grandparents in Washington state's Yakima Valley, life began anew in July 1939, when she stepped off the Alaska steamship *Denali* onto a lightering vessel and then onto the beaches of Nome.

"I walked down those dusty old roads past those ramshackle buildings and I just felt like I had come home," Bullock recalls. "It was a tremendous feeling. You felt like you were walking back in history."

Recently divorced and ready for a change, Bullock had eagerly accepted the invitation of her aunt and uncle, Emery and Grace Mahan, to live with them in Nome and a week earlier had left her Seattle home, and her conventional life, for the trip north. Her traveling companions had been several Filipino cannery workers who got off the ship at Dutch Harbor, a group of schoolteachers on a round-trip voyage from Seattle to Siberia and several Eskimos, whom Bullock mistakenly took for Japanese. She was 36 — for years, accounts of her life have incorrectly listed her age then as 33 — and ready for adventure.

Though immediately smitten with her new home, Bullock's initial introduction to this gold-crazed mining town was brief. A day after landing, she was on her way by truck and hand-pulled ferry to a remote mining camp six miles up the Solomon River. Working as a bookkeeper for Lee Brothers Dredging Co., Bullock remained at the site 40 miles outside

A veteran of more than 50 years in Alaska, the late Edith Bullock became a potent force in the commercial and political life of northwestern Alaska. (Courtesy of Marie Heinrichs)

Nome until late November. A half century later, she still remembers the moonlit, end-of-the-season truck ride back to town along the beach and around Cape Nome as among the most beautiful of her life.

That first winter in Nome was exciting. "Everything was so new and different," with time spent socializing and working as a stenographer for the Miners and Merchants Bank. Years later, Bullock would serve on the bank's board of directors. She returned to the Solomon River mine the following summer and in December 1940, married dredgemaster Jack Bullock in a simple ceremony at the home of her aunt and uncle. Then war broke out. Jack was drafted into the Army in 1941 and served the next three years as an Alaska Scout stationed in the Aleutians. Edith remained at home. She worked at the bank and, for a time, for the Bureau of Indian Affairs' reindeer service, which oversaw the territory's reindeer industry. In stolen moments she pored over agency reports and the writings of pioneer schoolteachers, learning all she could about the area and its Eskimo people.

With Jack finally home from the Aleutians, winters frequently were spent trapping in the upper Salcha River country outside Fairbanks. Long summer days found the Bullocks mining along northwestern Alaska's Kobuk River or outside Teller on the Seward Peninsula. "We just got by," says Bullock of those early years, "but it was a tremendous experience."

Now, when she closes her eyes and thumbs through mental snapshots collected during more than five decades in the North, it is images such as of a

shared trapping trip with Jack, their friend Chuck O'Leary and her black Labrador retriever, Teddy, that provide Bullock with some of her fondest memories. "It was just magnificent," she says of the months spent living in an isolated 11-by-11-foot cabin and cooking on a squat Yukon stove. "You really got down to the essentials of life. It was almost a spiritual experience."

It was during one of Jack's winter trapping trips that Edith was called to Kotzebue to fill in for a Wien Air Alaska employee out with a new baby. Edith and the townspeople clicked immediately. "They were real characters and Archie Ferguson was the main one," says Edith of the legendary business owner. "It was just fascinating.... We lived in a constant sideshow.

"It was really a Native town. It wasn't a white man's town," says Bullock, and that appealed to her. "I liked Kotzebue better than Nome. People didn't discriminate against anyone. We were all friends and acquaintances.

"Kotzebue was just really loads of fun. You just couldn't bear to miss a day. You'd go to Archie's lunch counter for a cup of coffee and all the gossip."

Intrigued with the town and its gentle, resourceful people, the Bullocks left Nome in 1948 and moved north, above the Arctic Circle, to Kotzebue.

"And that," says Edith, "was really the biggest change in my life."

On a table between the armchair and the sofa, Bullock tenderly turns the pages of a photo album. Its cover is of soft reindeer skin; its construction paper

A member of the Territorial Legislature from 1953 to 1958, Edith Bullock talks with legislators Charlie Fagerstrom (left) and Ted Duffield. Fagerstrom (1905-1962), born at Golovin Bay on Norton Sound, worked in construction and mining when the Legislature wasn't in session. An aviator originally from Nebraska, Duffield managed the Alaska Airlines station in Nome for several years in the 1940s and 1950s. Both Fagerstrom and Duffield were Democrats, Bullock a Republican. (Anchorage Museum of History and Art, Photo No. B88.57.4)

pages are brittle with age. The black-and-white snapshots, now faded, are the only tangible images that remain from Bullock's days on wind-swept Kotzebue Sound. A house fire in February 1958 destroyed everything and claimed the lives of a beloved Inupiat Eskimo friend

Archie Ferguson rests his hand on the propellor of his 1937 Cessna Airmaster at Kotzebue. Archie and his brother, Warren, began trading at Shungnak in the Kobuk Valley, then moved to Kotzebue where they consolidated their commercial empire. Warren drowned when his truck went through the ice on the lagoon behind Kotzebue. Archie continued the business and was a major factor in the economy of northwestern Alaska when the Bullocks arrived in Kotzebue in 1948. Edith and her husband, Jack, worked for a time for Ferguson, in an atmosphere Edith describes as "a constant sideshow." (Burley Putnam, Alaska Aviation Heritage Museum)

and of the Bullock's faithful dog. Now, years later, each photo brings to mind a ready story. There, for example, is one of Gust Carlson, Alice Connolly and others singing "Red River Valley" at one of the many parties held in the Bullock's spacious home. Carlson worked for the Bullocks and Connolly was a nurse in Kotzebue. And there's one from the Christmas party in the living room of the public health hospital in 1951 and of children trick-or-treating through the B & R office one Halloween. Beneath another is the caption "Hollywood Comes to Kotzebue — Lola Albright & Alan Hale." There's a photo of Art Flatt, the hospital maintenance engineer, participating in traditional Christmas games, of local residents butchering a beluga whale and skinning a polar bear and of hunters setting out on a trip up the Noatak River. Toward the back of the album are photos of tugs and barges, including the *Blue Fox* loaded with petroleum products ready for delivery to villages along the Kobuk River, of the new B & R barge No. 5 and of crews lightering an Alaska steamship. It is this group of photos that prompts Bullock to recount her days as one of Alaska's earliest and perhaps most successful businesswomen.

After moving in 1948 to Kotzebue, both Edith and Jack went to work for Archie Ferguson. Edith worked in the haphazard office Archie ran. Jack operated the tugboat. Tired of working for someone else, Jack came to Edith three years later with an announcement that would chart the course of both their lives: "I think we'll go into the barge business."

"Jack thought there was a great need for a lightering business and there was," explains Bullock of the decision to go into business for themselves. "Archie was so undependable.... He was not a businessman."

In addition to ferrying supplies onto the beach from ships anchored as many as 13 miles offshore in shallow Kotzebue Sound, Jack Bullock also saw a need for a company willing to haul fuel and other goods through the sound and upriver to Native villages along the Kobuk and Noatak. With Jack's experience as a tugboat operator, a loan from the bank in Nome and the use of Kotzebue storekeeper Louis Rotman's good name to secure credit, the Bullocks opened B & R Tug and Barge. That same year, 1951, Standard Oil of California built three tanks in Kotzebue, one each for gasoline, diesel fuel and stove oil. B & R

served as local distributors. The Bullocks hired Inupiat workers, found them to be dedicated employees and excellent seamen and, for the first time in Kotzebue, paid them in cash rather than with wooden tokens or store credit as had been the practice. "We didn't believe in controlling the Natives," says Bullock of the decision to pay their employees with cash long before there was even a bank in Kotzebue. "We felt they'd been taken advantage of by everyone," To fulfill their pledge, cash was flown in from Nome until a Kotzebue branch opened in 1960.

Rotman quickly tired of the problems that came with running a fledgling business and wanted out. Edith took over his interests. Two years later, a beleaguered Ferguson sold his barge company to the Bullocks, leaving them with a monopoly. Demand for their services escalated. The work was constant. Alaska steamships and government supply ships had to be unloaded to outlying villages before freezeup. Warehouses were built. Boats were taken out of the water by October with maintenance done through the winter and into spring. "We were," Bullock says quite simply, "terribly busy."

Once the business was established, Jack Bullock was away much of the time, working with Black Navigation Co. out of Fairbanks. [Black Navigation was a pioneering river freighting outfit on the Tanana and lower Yukon rivers.] Later Jack worked away from Kotzebue as a partner in the Nenana-based Yutana Barge Lines. Edith was left to manage B&R. The couple drifted apart. In 1966 they agreed to an amicable divorce. Edith,

who had served as company president since 1960, got B & R; Jack received their share of Yutana Barge Lines. "There were no hard feelings or bitterness," Bullock says of the eventual divorce. "He was an exciting man. He was the dreamer, the planner, and I was the organized one."

Jack Bullock eventually moved Outside. He died a couple of years ago in California.

Eighteen years after starting B & R, Edith decided in 1969 to sell what she proudly refers to as her mom and pop business. A $200,000 loan acquired five years earlier had been paid off. Though she had thoroughly enjoyed running the business, she was ready for the next phase of her life. "There's a time to do things and a time to let go," says Bullock of her decision to sell out to Pacific Inland Navigation. "I was ready to go."

It's been more than 20 years since Bullock was last in Kotzebue, though she still stays in touch with many there who made her years on the Baldwin Peninsula among her most cherished. For her 90th birthday on April 11, 1993, she received 126 cards, one of which was from Kotzebue and was signed by 20 of her old friends. And in winter of 1993, as is their habit, Bullock and a group of other former Kotzebue residents entered the Nenana Ice Classic, in which ticket purchasers guess when the ice will break up on the Tanana River at Nenana each spring. For the first time in 30 years, they were among the winners, with each receiving a check for $2,500.

Bullock, who still spends most mornings at her desk, writing to friends and former associates, initially planned to use her winnings to buy her first personal computer. On second thought, she decided a new typewriter would suit her needs just fine.

And although she keeps as busy as her health will allow, Bullock's days are now spent primarily at home, surrounded by tangible reminders of her days as a pioneering businesswoman and politician. Though weak and often tired, her face comes alive and her soft voice gathers strength when she talks about her earlier years in Alaska, years spent mining, running B & R, entertaining friends and visiting politicians and traveling among Kotzebue, Juneau and places Outside.

"It always pleased me when people asked me about the North," says Bullock. "I was an authority on that and that was fun for me.

"I felt we were living history all the time."

Looking back on her more than 50 years in Alaska, Bullock has no regrets. "I'm very grateful," says Bullock. "I've had a wonderful life." ■

Renowned sled dog racer George Attla kicks his way along the course through Fairbanks during the North American sled dog race. Attla, originally from Huslia in the Interior, has won many sprint races. The movie Spirit of the Wind is the story of his early life and his racing career. (Michael R. Speaks)

Hank Kroll on the drum, Mervin Brun on the mandolin and Orin Dimond on the guitar play for a social gathering in Seldovia in 1950. Before television, or even radio, in Seldovia, such get-togethers were common. This trio was well-known throughout lower Cook Inlet and the Kodiak area. (William Wakeland)

Julius Henry

By Bill Sherwonit

The truck in Julius Henry's yard is a strange sight indeed. Strange, because he lives in Platinum, a remote Eskimo village in southwest Alaska with about 40 inhabitants.

Main street through Platinum is less than a mile long though the road continues several miles out of town. All the neighbors are within easy walking distance and the nearest store is a few hundred yards from Henry's home. Not much reason to own a car or truck.

Here, four-wheelers and sno-gos capable of tundra, beach and mountain travel are the primary means of transport.

But Henry, who didn't see his first motor vehicle until his midteens, wanted a truck. Several years ago, he had one shipped from Anchorage to Bethel, at a cost of about $2,000. Then, in winter, he drove it nearly 150 miles cross-country following snow machine trails.

Now the truck mostly sits in his yard, used occasionally for work or pleasure. But Henry doesn't mind. It's simply one of his lifestyle's many oddities.

Like his neighbors, Henry lives in a prefab house with few modern amenities. Instead of telephones, there are CB radios. Instead of toilets and plumbing, there are honey buckets that must be dumped. Water must be hauled daily from a well and wood must be chopped for the stove.

Village homes do have electricity, which supplies power for lights, TV and even VCRs. Though he watches his share of videos and satellite-beamed television, Henry worries about their impact on village ways.

"The tube has changed our lifestyle," he says. "When I was little, the kids collected water and dumped honey buckets for their family and elders before going to school. Now... it's just not the same."

Born Jan. 4, 1949, at Quinhagak, an Eskimo community about 70 miles north of Platinum on the Bering Sea coast,

Henry moved to his present home in 1980 after traveling outside Alaska for schooling and National Guard training.

The village was named after a nearby platinum deposit found in 1926 by an Eskimo, Water Smith. That discovery led to a local boom, but Platinum never grew large; its population reportedly peaked at 72 in 1950.

While mining had its heyday, the Bering Sea's marine riches have proved more important to the long-term well-being of Platinum's Eskimo residents. Like many Natives who live along the southwest coast, Henry commercial fishes in summer and leads a largely subsistence lifestyle the rest of the year. Meals often include local fish and wildlife — salmon, waterfowl, ptarmigan, caribou — supplemented by groceries bought at the village store. A popular dessert is Eskimo ice cream, a mix of berries, jelly, sugar and Crisco oil.

Since 1991, Henry has also served as a village health aide, responsible for meeting Platinum's day-to-day medical

needs. He volunteered for training when the previous health aide threatened to quit if she didn't get some help.

She eventually left her position anyway, leaving Henry as Platinum's only local health-care provider.

"It's stressful," he admits. "I have to be on call 24 hours a day — and it seems the emergencies usually happen at night. The worst part is feeling alone, that all the responsibilities are on my shoulders."

Henry operates out of a clinic built in the mid-1980s. Most of his patients are children with earaches or colds, but occasionally he must deal with severe traumas, from broken bones to gunshot wounds. His busiest season is May through July, when hundreds of

Among the most isolated of Alaska's many Bush communities is Platinum, a tiny settlement on the Bering Sea coast south of Bethel. Julius Henry makes his home here, where he commercial fishes in season and spends the rest of the time living a subsistence lifestyle. (Mark Dolan)

commercial fishermen come for the annual herring harvest. Inevitably, accidents occur that require his help.

"Sometimes I feel like quitting," he admits, "but I won't until there's someone to take my place. The people here put a lot of faith in health aides; out here, we're so far from 911 that the health aide is everything." ■

Carl Jensen

By Bill Sherwonit

Sled dog teams were rural Alaska's primary wintertime mail carriers for more than a quarter century, until replaced by airplanes in the 1920s and '30s. But in a few isolated corners of the state, mushing mail carriers continued to make their appointed rounds into the 1950s and '60s. One of the last was Carl Jensen.

Born in 1928 at Old Iliamna, a now-deserted Athabaskan village along the Iliamna River, Jensen drove a mail-delivery dog team from 1948 to 1954, when the U.S. Postal Service canceled his contract.

"I've heard that I was one of the last two people in Alaska to deliver mail by dog team in 1954," he says. "The Postal Service pretty much outlawed hauling mail by dogs after that. They said airplanes were safer and provided better service. I agreed, actually; planes could cover in one hour what might take me two weeks."

Carl took over the route from his father, Mike Jensen Sr., whose many years of mail service ended when he contracted tuberculosis.

Mike Jensen's initial contract required that he meet the mailboat twice a year at Iliamna Bay, then carry the mail over a traditional portage route connecting Cook Inlet with Lake Iliamna. His route was substantially modified in 1940, to reflect changing times; Mike would meet a plane at Iliamna, then deliver the mail to the lake communities of Igiugig, Pile Bay and Pedro Bay.

Carl inherited his dad's route at age 20, after a lengthy absence from the Iliamna region. He'd gone away in 1941 to attend school at Cordova and eventually ended up in Petersburg, working as the fireman on a drill barge. He returned home at his father's request.

"Dad was dying," Carl recalls. "He wanted me to take care of the family. I had to do it."

Taking care of family business also meant delivering mail. Like his father, Carl usually worked on a nine-month contract that required mail runs every two weeks, from March through December. He traveled by boat when Iliamna Lake was open and by dog team when it froze.

The hardest times were the in-between periods, when boat travel was impossible but weak ice prevented a safe lake crossing; then he'd have to go overland. Short, routine runs across the lake were replaced by difficult passages through forested hills. The trip from Iliamna to Pile Bay, only 45 miles by boat, was 70 up-and-down miles overland. A complete circuit that would take two days with the lake frozen, might instead take two weeks.

"Sometimes there was no snow," he says, "so I had to drive the team across bare ground. Other times I got caught in stormy weather and deep snow so bad you couldn't move; I did my share of camping in blizzards. But I went regardless of the trail conditions, or the weather. The mail had to be delivered."

Jensen used a 12-foot-long freight sled,

pulled by 12 to 14 malamute huskies — the most he could easily handle — to carry his mail load, usually weighing 700 to 800 pounds, plus survival gear: food, extra layers of cold-weather clothing and a large tarp for shelter.

Weighing 80 to 90 pounds, the malamutes were bred and raised as work dogs. Besides hauling mail they were also used for hunting, trapping and general transportation.

Chief among Jensen's kennel of 35 to 40 dogs were several reliable leaders he trained himself. And the best of the best was Clancy: "long-legged, fast and a dog that would really listen to commands."

"I don't know how he did it, but he'd always lead you home, even if it was pitch-black, in a blizzard," Jensen says. "I'd just let Clancy go, let him have his head, and he'd get us there. Or if I fell off the sled and lost the team, all I had to do was holler and he'd bring 'em right back."

Local residents naturally greeted Jensen's arrivals with open arms.

A man of many hats, Carl Jensen was called back from Southeast to his native region of Iliamna when his father contracted tuberculosis. Carl took over his father's mail delivery contract, using sled dogs to deliver the mail to villages along Lake Iliamna. When more modern transportation prompted the U.S. Postal Service to cancel his contract, Carl and his wife, Marge, branched out to provide a variety of services from their Pedro Bay home. Among those services is a new contract with the U.S. Postal Service, this time to run the post office at Pedro Bay. (Mark Dolan)

"I was the most welcome person at any village," he says with a chuckle, "mainly because they only got their mail twice a month. I was welcome at most any house, and usually would stay with a family."

Jensen, who's lived since 1950 at Pedro Bay, a small Dena'ina Athabaskan Indian village at Lake Iliamna's east end, had no problem adapting when his mail-delivery contract ended in '54. A multitalented man, he's worked at a variety of jobs during the last 40 years. At present, he and wife, Marge — they've been married "a bunch of years," since 1960 — operate Triple K Services, named after children Kevin, Karla and Keith. Among the

services they offer: a bed-and-breakfast; sport fish and big-game guiding; freight hauling; wood chopping; and "just about anything else a person might need."

To keep from getting bored, Carl also fishes commercially and does contract work as a heavy equipment operator, electrician and telephone company technician.

One other thing: Carl Jensen again owns a contract with the U.S. Postal Service. "Not as a carrier," he says smiling. "Now all I do is run the local post office."

And yes, he still owns dogs. But these days, they're only pets. ∎

Roland Lee left a British ship that had stopped at the Homer Spit. He retired to die, suffering from, among other things, a prostate problem, a common ailment among those who drink a lot of tea. He found a spot near Fritz Creek on a low bluff overlooking Kachemak Bay. There, close to the edge so it would fall over the cliff in a year or two and leave no sign, he built a hut. He made it largely of long-stemmed, red-top grass to resemble the huts he'd seen on South Pacific islands. But his health improved so he built another hut a little farther back from the cliff. When this photo was taken in 1947, he was in his third hut, a substantial little building of wood from which he communicated with the world by short-wave radio and Morse code. (William Wakeland)

Bill and Lill Fickus
Brooks Range Homesteaders

By Roger Kaye

Life was hard when Lill Fickus was growing up. A Gwitch'in Athabaskan, Lill's roots are in Arctic Village, Alaska's farthest north and perhaps most traditional Indian community. Subsistence was the focus of her childhood; the labors of the quest for food were unremitting. But she looks back on mostly happy times, extended family trips by dog team and living at caribou camp in the hills south of the village.

One lasting memory of camp life is when as a little girl she tried to help her family trap ground squirrels. Everyone was catching some but Lill. She was discouraged. Finally one afternoon, she found a squirrel in one of her traps. "I was so happy and proud, I still remember my father shout, 'Oh, you caught one.'" Only years later did Lill learn that he had surreptitiously placed the squirrel in her trap. And only after becoming a parent did she appreciate the lesson of that event.

When she was 14, Lill went to Mount Edgecumbe High School in Sitka and took training in nursing. Later she found a job as a nurse and secretary in Fort Yukon, where she met a dashing flier.

For about as long as he can remember, Bill Fickus wanted to go to Alaska and become a bush pilot. He grew up in rural Pennsylvania, where as a teenager he worked weekends steering a plow behind a horse and helping as a general handyman.

In 1956, Bill moved to Alaska and began an air taxi business with a small, fabric-covered Piper. While prospecting in the Brooks Range that winter, he landed his ski-equipped plane near the confluence of Crevice Creek and the John

More than 30 years ago Lill Fickus introduced her husband to her childhood love of roasting caribou ribs over an open fire. They regularly climb the foothills behind the homestead for a cookout. (Roger Kaye)

The Fickus family ranch sits on the north bank of Crevice Creek, 70 miles north of the Arctic Circle. (Roger Kaye)

River. Here were prospects for gold, and he liked the country.

The new Alaskan married his Indian sweetheart in 1959. They worked mining claims along Crevice Creek for four summers. Then, with a daughter, 3, they decided to make the mining camp a permanent home.

The challenge of their isolated homestead, 40 miles north of Bettles, led them to become an industrious, multitalented, self-reliant couple. Subsistence hunting, guiding, ranching, gardening, mining, trapping and skin-sewing have been their livelihood. Their varied undertakings required working together as a family, a need they look back upon as the foundation of their four grown children's success.

Situated on the forested floor of the mountainous John River valley, the Fickus family homestead and surrounding fields look like a calendar picture of a Swiss farm, except for the nearby airplane and runway.

Small-scale gold mining has been a main source of income. During the short high-water season, Bill camps at the mine, located several miles up the creek. A miner at age 10, youngest son, Tim, remembers his pride in helping with odd jobs and later running the suction dredge. "As kids, our work was our play," he says.

For Bill, if there is hardship to life here, it's when things mechanical break down.

"Whatever breaks, we have to fix it ourselves. We learn from manuals, but mostly through trial and error — and there's lots of error," Bill says.

Necessity and a small but well-equipped machine shop provide almost everything needed for improvisation. Sometimes though, a critical item like a hydraulic fitting cannot be repaired or built. Real hardship, Bill says, "is when you need one piddly little part and have to fly 250 miles to Fairbanks to get it."

By 1965, the mining was not providing enough income to support the growing family. Bill became a registered hunting guide and Lill an assistant guide. Each fall, using horses, they led hunters in search of Dall sheep, bear, moose and caribou. About half their clients have been Europeans. "Guiding non-English speakers is the most fun," Lill laughs. "It's a week-long game of playing charades."

Often the clients become lifelong friends. One such hunter, Lill recalls, was Johnnas von Trapp, whose family was featured in "The Sound of Music." After shooting his sheep, von Trapp helped Lill cut up the meat. Then, to his confusion, she salvaged parts of the animal he couldn't imagine edible.

"I told him I go by my Native way," Lill says. "When we get done there won't be enough for a camp robber [gray jay] to get a full meal." Back at camp, he tried her sheep-gut soup, and liked it.

Working with clients was both education and employment for the children. They were paid $20 a trip to take care of the horses, set up camp and pack. "I never give my kids money for nothing," Lill says. "I always want them to learn to earn."

In lean times, when the Fickuses were eligible for government assistance, they turned it down. During visits to the villages, their children played with others who could buy things because their families had accepted welfare. Comparisons were inevitable.

"One time my kids ask, 'How come they get money and we don't?'" Lill recalls. "I told 'em we don't believe in welfare, it makes people lazy.... The government don't help us because we can do it all by ourselves."

The expense of feeding the horses led Bill to clear 35 acres of forest to grow hay. He drove a 1942 Case tractor up the frozen John River from Bettles [accessible by river barge], then fashioned a three-bladed plow from a curved birch tree and parts scavenged from old mining equipment. They planted timothy grass and experimented with various strains of oats, wheat and barley, later harvested with a homemade thrashing machine. The family raised cows, horses, hogs, goats, geese and chickens. For several years grain and produce from an expansive garden were sold to villages. In three years the Crevice Creek homestead became what the *Guinness Book of Records* declared the northernmost ranch in the United States.

As farming, mining and hunting give way to the long season of cold and darkness, the Fickuses' seasonal cycle turns to trapping and indoor projects.

With the children gone now, Bill and Lill run about 40 miles of trap line, specializing in lynx, marten, fox and wolverine. The snow machine, having replaced their dog team, enables them to run the trap line without overnighting in tent camps. Until spring, Lill does skin-

Edison Williams, visiting from Allakaket, watches Bill Fickus cut up Jenny, a horse that died during a January cold spell. The meat will be used for dog food. (Roger Kaye)

sewing; making mukluks, mittens, beaded slippers, bracelets, belts and necklaces for sale in town.

"Winter is a dangerous time for people prone to TV addiction," Lill says while working on a pair of slippers. It is hard to visualize her lean frame passively parked in front of a tube.

"Oh, I watch it when we're visiting town," she says, "so I know what we're not missing. People complain that the shows are no good, or they're bad for their kids, or it takes too much of their time."

"Doesn't yours have a turn-off button?" I asked her.

"If a TV started controlling my life," she adds, "I'd take it out and shoot it."

With the children gone, Bill and Lill's needs have decreased; the trap line is a few miles shorter now and the scope of other endeavors has been reduced.

"Of all the things we've done out here," Lill recalls, "the hardest for me was when we put our first child, Debbie, in the plane to go off to high school. I worried for her. Then I knew what my mother felt when I left the village to go to school."

In 1980, Debbie Fickus was named Miss Alaska. In turn, Matt, Linda and Tim have left for high school, and gone on to become successful adults with good jobs.

Lill attributes her and Bill's parenting accomplishments to "providing a Christian home, teaching by example and keeping the kids busy working with the family." Recalling early experiences like squirrel trapping, she feels the greatest gift of her childhood was the sense of responsibility she earned through knowing her contribution to the family was always needed.

"That's what I tried to pass on to my kids," she says, "and not let them learn their values and waste their life in front of a TV." ∎

Lloyd Pederson

By Sean Reid

Editor's note: *Sean is a free-lance writer from Anchorage.*

Petersburg. Take a guided tour through this picturesque southeastern Alaska community, and you'll most likely visit the fish hatchery, the museum and nearby LeConte Glacier. You'll probably even see Lloyd Pederson and his 1964 Rambler station wagon.

Pederson, a lifelong Petersburg resident, and his uniquely adorned Rambler have become genuine tourist attractions.

Nasturtiums, a thermometer, inflated California raisin toys, deflated and severed fishing floats, an artificial swan, other fishing paraphernalia and assorted signs and stickers offering commentary on a multitude of subjects adorn Lloyd Pederson's 1964 Rambler station wagon in Petersburg. (Sean Reid)

Jack Carson, in his early 70s when the photographer met him in 1948, lived along the beach between Cape Yakataga and Icy Bay. He and his partner, Carl Killion, maintained several cabins and lived off the land. Jack had had an adventurous life in Alaska including prospecting in the Wrangell Mountains and working on the Copper River & Northwestern Railroad that ran from Cordova to the Kennicott Copper Mine in the Wrangell Mountains. Jack and Carl hunted, trapped, gardened and recovered gold from the beach. They maintained a system of ditches directing water seasonally over a section of beach. At the proper time in the summer, they set up a sluice box, and using water from the ditch system, they concentrated the gold. These tailings were then panned to recover the fine gold that had washed up from a marine source and been concentrated in the little gulleys created by the ditches. Dogs, mostly setters, played a key role in the survival of the pair, providing virtually the only means of transport, either as shown here or hitched to carts pulled along the beach. Asked why he lived here, Jack responded: "A man gets old too damn soon Outside. Why, a fellow can't get out and walk without fear of being bumped off by a car." (William Wakeland)

"I enjoy seeing all the smiles this car brings to tourists," says Pederson, who deliberately cruises the downtown streets. "And I guess the Chamber of Commerce thinks it's a pretty good thing because they've paid a few of my parking tickets."

The "flower car," as Pederson likes to refer to his mobile creation, began life much like any other automobile. But one day in the early 1970s, Pederson hung an old rubber float on the side of his car.

As time went on, the car began to assume a new identity. Friends increasingly saw fit to donate all forms of memorabilia, flora, flotsam and jetsam.

Now the car has acquired a loosely artistic appearance of mixed media.

December and August are particularly good times to enjoy Pederson's Rambler. "It shows up real well here in the snow with its Christmas tree and lights," says the proud owner. "Of course, it shows up real well in full summer bloom, too." Hundreds of nasturtiums grow in season in exterior flower boxes and adorn the car's top. "Those flower boxes were made from lumber taken from the fish-hold of a boat," Pederson said.

Pederson loves boats. In fact, he may owe as much of his fame to boats as to his Rambler. Nationwide, viewers of

television, especially sports fans regularly exposed to beer commercials, might remember Pederson's boat, the *Middleton*, as one of the props in Old Milwaukee® beer's "Glacier Bay, Alaska" advertisement that ran a few years ago.

Stardom escaped Pederson, who did not appear in the ad. Quips Pederson, "The producers didn't want an old coot like me in the commercial.... They wanted young beer drinkers."

Through his dry humor shines the youthful spirit of this man of 72 years. He sold his boat, but he says, "I don't think I'd ever sell the Rambler....the kids around town really like it." ■

Frieda and Ignatius Kosbruk

By Bill Sherwonit

A midwinter storm is blasting the Alaska Peninsula coast with gale-force winds and wet snow, typical February weather for this part of the world, as Frieda and Ignatius Kosbruk welcome guests into their home.

Sitting in their small but comfortable kitchen, the Kosbruks generously share coffee, fried bread and stories from their past.

Married 47 years, Frieda and Ignatius are lifelong residents of Perryville, an Alutiiq community, population about 100, which was settled in 1912 by people fleeing the eruption of Mount Katmai.

Frieda was born in 1916, Ignatius the following year. They married in the late 1940s after Frieda's first husband, John, died from tuberculosis. Frieda also lost a baby boy, Nick, to TB. Other deadly illnesses such as influenza and pneumonia also periodically swept through the village.

"We used to watch them dying from fever," Ignatius says. "We didn't know what to do."

Sickness wasn't the only hardship, he adds: "In the old days, the people used to be very, very poor. There was a lack of doctors, lack of food. I used to pack meat and stuff 16 hours a day, all on foot, to feed my family. It was hard times."

Things are easier now. Homes have electricity and plumbing. Nearly every family owns a four-wheeler and a TV. There's even a village store and health clinic. Plus a church and school, of course.

Perryville actually got its first school long ago, back in 1923. But as in most Alaska Native communities, the arrival of western education proved to be a mixed blessing. "They didn't allow us to speak in our own tongue," Frieda says. "They spank us or have us stand in the corner."

Adds Ignatius, "Now, after 60 years, they want the culture back. But that's very, very difficult to do."

Ignatius and Frieda held onto their language despite the punishments, and they weave both Alutiiq and English into conversations. But daughters Liz and Vivian Kosbruk have difficulty speaking Alutiiq, though they can at least understand their Native tongue.

Before the arrival of western teachers and doctors, villagers depended on "herbs from the ground" for both food and medicine. The roots of wild geraniums, locally known as candle flowers, were used to heal sore throats, for example.

FACING PAGE: Ignatius and Frieda Kosbruk have seen many changes in their combined century and a half of living on the Alaska Peninsula. They make their home at Perryville, an Alutiiq settlement tucked into a corner of the mainland between Mitrofania and Ivanof bays along the peninsula's Pacific coast. Commercial fishing dominates the community's economy and each fishing season sees an exodus to the Chignik area, center of a thriving fishery. (Mark Dolan)

"You take the roots, crush them, and put them on a clean cloth," Frieda says. "Then you boil some water, run it through the cloth. And after it cools, you use it for gargle. It takes a couple days; it clears out the phlegm."

Some plants, such as wormwood, are still used today. Rubbed on the back while taking steam baths, it helps to ease aching muscles.

Traditional Alutiiq healers such as Frieda's deceased uncle, Wasco Sanook, also used a technique called bloodletting. As the Kosbruks explain: "First you take the flesh and squeeze it together, then you hold it from the other side and the doctor pokes (his knife) through your flesh. That's the best medicine the people ever had. For poor blood, or tuberculosis, or anything. They let it all drain out and keep that wound open for a week or so. After about three or four days, the person get well.

"Anytime the person get pain, they use the knife to cut it open. I'll tell you where we used to get it: right here, between the shoulders. If I pinch you, it hurt, that's where they put the knife through. All the black (bad blood) coming out . . . That's the best medicine we used to use."

Despite their fondness for traditional cures, the Kosbruks appreciate modern medicines as well. White doctors helped Ignatius with both ulcers and a smoking addiction: "The doctor at Dillingham told me I'm gonna die if I don't stop smoking; he took pictures of my lungs, and showed me all the nicotine spots. I was worried, but the doctor sent me pills to help; I took one, and it helped me stop. That was about 10 years ago."

As for Perryville's health clinic, run by Liz and Vivian, Ignatius says, "We never had anything like that in the old days. It's very, very good." ∎

Sigurd T. Olson

By Bruce H. Baker

Editor's note: *Bruce is a forest resource consultant and free-lance writer.*

It was one of those clear, crisp winter days when crystals of hoar frost glistened, the peaks of the Juneau Icefield could be seen in the background, and the snow compressed lightly beneath our skis. I commented to Sig Olson that he'd been making ski tracks for a long time. He grinned and told how one day he was riding up the Eaglecrest chairlift near Juneau with a youngster about 10. To make conversation, Sig asked him how long he'd been skiing. The boy proudly said, "About four years, how about you?" Sig reflected momentarily and answered modestly, "Oh, at least 60 years." The boy didn't respond but his face revealed an uncomprehending look.

That was about five years ago, and Sig is still at it. To Juneauites, he has become a sort of skiing legend. Skiers of all ages admire his ability to link turn after turn through deep, untracked powder snow. Aspiring skiers wish they could ski as well, and fellow powder-hounds hope they'll be able to "ski the deep" when they're Sig's age. Even on the groomed ski runs, one had better have their skis well waxed if they're to keep up with him.

Born in 1923, Sig was skiing by age 5 in Ely, Minn. He and his friends ski jumped with long wooden skis, the kind that draw a nostalgic glance when mounted crosswise on the wall of a ski lodge. There's a runout slope at Eaglecrest where it's safe to get one's body into a low, aerodynamic tuck and let the skis run free. After one such run, we were speculating on how fast we thought we'd been travelling. Sig said, "The fastest I've ever gone on skis is 84 miles an hour." As a youth, he was skiing behind a car on a lake near Ely. "It was so cold that it felt like I wasn't wearing any clothes. I never have told my folks about that."

Ely is the jump-off point for canoe travel in northern Minnesota and adjacent Ontario. In the summertime, Sig's skiing gave way to guiding canoe trips for Border Lakes Outfitters, a business established by his father and a partner. His father was Sigurd F. Olson, teacher, outdoor writer and wilderness advocate. Sigurd T's youthful experiences made a deep impression on him, and a visit to his home will reveal plenty of memorabilia including books and artwork relating to wilderness, wildlife, history and exploration of the North Country. Loons, those ancient birds that have become a symbol of the lake country, were the subject of his graduate thesis.

With his experience, it was natural that Sig would end up becoming a skiing and rock climbing instructor in the 10th Mountain Division when it trained in the mountains of Colorado. The 10th made a name for itself in the Apennine Mountains of Italy during World War II. By piecing together what has been written about the unit with the occasional recollection that Sig shares—he doesn't talk about it much—one can begin to appreciate what the 10th went through. It's been reported that in the 114 days that the division was in combat, 992 of its men were lost and another 4,154 wounded out of the total 14,000 who were mobilized. The 10th is said to have borne the heaviest casualties of any division for the length of time in combat in World War II.

Several years back, the K2 ski company put out commemorative skis featuring the name and insignia of the 10th Mountain Division that were made available to veterans of that unit. Sig is justifiably proud of the pair he received, and anyone hoping to see them show up at an annual ski swap will probably have a long wait. After the war, Sig earned a master's degree in wildlife management, and he, his wife, and two sons came to Alaska in 1951. He worked for more than 30 years here as a wildlife biologist, first with the U.S. Fish and Wildlife Service, then the new state of Alaska, and later, the U.S. Forest Service where he was appointed director of the Division of Wildlife Management and Fisheries. He's full of stories about what wildlife management in Alaska was like in the days before there were a half million Alaskans competing with the state's wildlife and when natural resource management agencies were more field and less office oriented than they are now.

Sig's public service comes full circle

When the slopes aren't suitable for skiing, Sigurd T. Olson takes his fly rod to the streams of Admiralty Island south of Juneau. Sig, as he is known to many, worked as a wildlife manager for various government agencies before retirement. (Mark Kelley)

back to skiing, and his active involvement on the National Ski Patrol spans 32 years. It began at Juneau's old "Third Cabin" rope tow and continued at Eaglecrest. He's only been retired from the ski patrol since 1991, and this past winter when looking for one last end-of-the-day run through the powder, Sig couldn't help comment to the ski patroller standing by to make the final check of the mountain, "You've got my old sweep."

Ski legs are best kept in condition on a year-round basis, and Sig works hard to keep his in shape. After the chairlift shuts down for the season in May, he can be found gaining the ridge with climbing skins on his skis, perhaps dropping one of his favorite quotes, "Climb the mountain like an old man; come down the mountain like a young man." From the

top, climbing skins removed, Sig makes graceful telemark turns down the slope, reminiscent of both his Nordic heritage and his youth when "that was the only turn we did." And when the snow's gone for the summer? Well, you're likely to hear Sig say, "I really had a great time rollerblading out North Douglas road last night. It was so quiet you could hear a car coming from a long way off, and there just weren't any."

I'm hearing this as Sig and I trek up into the alpine meadows of Granite Creek Basin, little more than a two-hour hike from the steps of the state Capitol in Juneau.

"Come over here a minute," Sig says as we walk along the trail under a sunny sky, separated by a few alder bushes from the loud torrent called Gold Creek. I snap my pup on a leash and follow Sig through the brush out on to one of the huge boulders around and over which the white water flows.

"The last time I had my parents out for a walk here in Alaska, they were able to come up the trail this far. We were standing right here when suddenly a female merganser and her brood came riding down the rapids."

"Right through the foam?" I ask.

"Yes," Sig says, "The water wasn't quite this high but almost. Then we saw them fly back upstream past us and do it all over again. That really made our day an adventure."

Sig tries to make every day an adventure, and whether it's skiing, canoeing, hiking, or bringing a coho salmon in with a fly rod, the experience will commonly end with a handshake and Sig's comment, "We did a good thing today." ∎

The forest industry has played an important role in Alaska's economy since Russian times. This forester trims logs at the Ketchikan Pulp Co. plant near Ward Cove north of Ketchikan. (Harry M. Walker)

Ernest N. Patty

By Stanton H. Patty

Editor's note: *Stanton H. Patty, born and reared in Fairbanks, is the retired assistant travel editor of* The Seattle Times. *Ernest and Kathryn Patty were his parents.*

It didn't take long for the young mining engineer to know that Alaska was where he belonged.

"It was something like falling in love," said Dr. Ernest N. Patty, pioneer mining man and educator.

Many years later, talking with his family, he recalled the moment: The year was 1923. Patty was mushing a dog team to check out a gold discovery in the wild country between Fairbanks and Mount McKinley. Suddenly, the mountain, soaring above the clouds, caught the blush of a rosy sunrise.

"So this is what Alaska is," he mused. "All at once I knew I wanted to be part of this country, so magnificent and so full of great promise."

Ernest Newton Patty (1894-1976) was part of Alaska for 40 years, first as a faculty member at the brand-new Alaska Agricultural College and School of Mines, later to be the University of Alaska, then as a successful mining operator in Alaska and Yukon Territory, and finally circling back to the university as its third president.

"There was always useful work to do and another summit just ahead," he said.

But the Alaska adventure began with what Patty later would call "a kind of reckless hope."

Patty, born in the eastern Oregon town of La Grande, was fresh out of the University of Washington and a stint with the Washington State Geological Survey when he met Dr. Charles E. Bunnell, first president of the new college in Fairbanks. Bunnell asked Patty to sign on as professor of geology and mineralogy at the college, which had only an empty building and big dreams.

"Dr. Bunnell fired our imaginations with tales of life in the Far North," Patty

remembered. "I suspected at the time that we had been oversold, that I had indeed gone off half-cocked when I agreed to take the job."

Ernest Patty, his wife, Kathryn, and their first-born son, Ernest, sailed north in September 1922 aboard the Alaska Steamship Co.'s S.S. *Northwestern*.

A fellow passenger, a blunt-talking businessman from Juneau, told Patty that he was making a mistake.

"I hope you bought a round-trip ticket, son, because you're sure as ---- going to need it," he said. "Trying to start a college at Fairbanks is a great blunder. I doubt it will even open its doors."

Patty felt his wife tremble as they stood at the rail and watched the ship thread the jade fiords of southeastern Alaska. "It was not the cold that made her shudder," he wrote years later. "My stout-hearted Kay was frightened.

"If at that moment I could have picked up our baby, taken my wife by the hand and walked home, I probably would have done it. Well, I thought, 'if we were off on

Ernest N. Patty, left, prepares for a winter flight out of Fairbanks. With him is Fred Parker, deputy U.S. marshal, in fur coat. At rear is famed pilot Joe Crosson, who history tapped twice for the grim task of retrieving the bodies of famous pilots who had crashed during the early years of Alaska aviation. Crosson and Harold Gillam found and returned the bodies of Carl Ben Eielson and his mechanic from Russia during an international search in 1929. In 1935 he brought back the bodies of Wiley Post and Will Rogers from their crash site near Barrow. (Courtesy of Stanton H. Patty)

a wild-goose chase, we might as well have as much fun as possible.'"

The little college opened Sept. 13, 1922, with a brave ceremony. Patty recalled how a clergyman's invocation called on God to permit the new institution to bring wonderful things to Alaska. "We certainly needed God's help," Patty said.

There were six faculty members — and only six students. "There was no danger that any student was going to be lost in the crowd," Patty said.

Before long, Patty was teaching mining and doing mining. On weekends and during summer recesses he explored prospects around the territory as a consultant for several mining companies. It was not uncommon for him to shoulder a heavy pack and set off alone to hike 100 miles or more across the wilderness.

There were long, and sometimes dangerous, days on the trail. One day, while climbing toward a mining prospect above Turnagain Arm, Patty was trapped in a snowslide. His scalp was gashed, and his right arm was broken. "There is nothing like a mountain to cut a man down to size," he said.

Often his wife would join him to travel the Yukon River country by boat and bush plane in search of new mining prospects. Kathryn Patty long since had shed her fears of life in Alaska.

In 1925, Patty was appointed dean of the college and head of the School of Mines, which quickly was gaining a reputation as one of the top mining schools in the United States. From then on it was Dean Patty, a nickname that became so well known around Alaska throughout the years that some thought Dean was his first name.

As a mining engineer, Ernest Patty was always looking for ways to more efficiently get minerals from the ground. One of his innovations was to remove the overburden from mineral-bearing gravels, thus enabling solar energy to thaw the ground and ease the task of collecting the gravels. Behind Patty, center, is the floating dredge at Woodchopper. Inside the dredge, buckets on a conveyor belt scooped up gravel and dumped it onto a series of screens that eventually sifted out the rock and allowed the gold to settle. (Courtesy of Stanton H. Patty)

Patty was an innovator, in the classroom and in the field. He decided to develop a novel form of adult education, a short course for prospectors who were roaming Alaska in search of gold. The more the miners knew about rocks that might be associated with ores, the better their chances of making a strike.

The project required some unusual teaching methods. Patty decided that poker might catch the men's interest. "These fellows, I knew, would be of various ages and backgrounds, but, as miners, they were sure to have one thing in common: a working knowledge of poker," he said.

So the professor devised a card game with rocks. Teams of players were dealt hands of numbered rocks such as granite, limestone and dolomite, then challenged to identify the specimens with each wager.

Things almost got out of hand during one session.

"What do you say, Prof, if we all ante in a dollar?" one student asked.

"Do you want me to lose my job?" Patty asked.

Teacher and students compromised by agreeing that the losing side would buy lunch that day for the winners.

As aviation was beginning to give Alaska wings, Patty decided to take to the air for field trips. This way the students could observe geological features that before had been only words and pictures in textbooks.

Patty enjoyed teaching, but was restless to get back into the mining industry on a full-time basis. "I wanted to see if I could still do the things I had been teaching," he said.

Into his life in 1934 came A. D. McRae, a hard-driving Vancouver, B.C. industrialist and World War I military leader. McRae believed Alaska had a golden future, and was looking to invest in northern mining properties. He hired Patty to go with him for a month and inspect some prospects.

The search was discouraging. McRae soon had spent more than $70,000 and had nothing to show for it. Patty was sure the Canadian would abandon the effort.

Then one day Patty happened to mention Coal Creek, a gold-flecked Yukon River tributary about 110 miles northeast of Fairbanks, where pick-and-shovel miners, most old-timers, were making meager livings. Perhaps, Patty said, a modern placer dredge could turn Coal Creek into a profitable venture.

"Charter a bush plane for morning," McRae ordered. "Let's go."

McRae and Patty liked what they found at Coal Creek and optioned several miles of ground from the claim-holders.

"This is your baby, Patty. I want you to run the show," McRae announced.

In 1935, Patty resigned from the university to become vice president and general manager of the Coal Creek venture, which was operating under the name Gold Placers, Inc. Soon McRae and his partners added a neighboring property, Woodchopper, calling that venture Alluvial Golds, Inc.

Big placer dredges were shipped in pieces to Coal Creek and Woodchopper, assembled and put to work. The first cleanup of the Coal Creek dredge yielded $27,000 in gold.

There was joy in camp that night. McRae and Patty rested in their tent, listening to the laughter of the crew. "Fine sounds to hear in a mining camp," Patty recalled.

Mining operations later were extended into Yukon Territory, near Dawson City, focal point of the fabled Klondike gold rush, then to Atlin, in British Columbia.

Rising production costs just after World War II, with the price of gold fixed at $35 an ounce, badly pinched Alaska's gold-mining industry. Ways had to be found to trim expenses.

It was then that Patty, the mining engineer, came up with an idea that helped rescue his own companies and other small dredge operators around the territory. He reasoned: Instead of using labor-intensive hydraulic nozzles to strip the overburden of muck atop possible gold-bearing gravels, why not try solar thawing? Why not remove a minimum of overburden and let the heat of the short-summer sun thaw the frozen gravel underneath for several seasons ahead. "We were letting nature do the work,"

Patty said with a grin.

Fate had a way of meeting Ernest Patty on northern trails.

In 1947, Ernest Patty Jr., oldest of the Pattys' three sons, was killed in an airplane crash near Woodchopper. The grieving parents, who had by then settled for winters in Seattle, began cutting their ties with Alaska.

"Alaska can be as cruel as it is beautiful," Patty said.

In 1953, the University of Alaska awarded Patty an honorary degree and invited him to be its commencement speaker. A few days later the university regents asked Patty to take over as president of the struggling institution.

"No, impossible," Patty responded. The regents said they would hold the position open for 60 days. A few days later Patty telegraphed his acceptance.

"I think I already had made a tentative commitment in my heart the first time I talked with the regents," he recalled.

Now, instead of mourning a lost son, the Pattys were taking on responsibility

Ernest Patty culminated his career in Alaska with an appointment as president of the University of Alaska from 1953 to 1960. His Wisconsin-born wife, Kathryn, shared her husband's nearly 40 years in Alaska. (Courtesy of Stanton H. Patty)

for hundreds of young persons on the Fairbanks campus where their Alaska adventure had begun long ago.

Patty stayed on as president until 1960, when Kathryn Patty's failing health caused him to resign.

"We have paid off part of the debt we owe to Alaska," Patty told his wife as they prepared to depart Fairbanks.

Their remaining time together was short. Mrs. Patty died of cancer the next year. Ernest Patty followed in 1976, at age 81.

The sons of Ernest and Kathryn Patty had lumps in their throats, and knowing smiles, whenever their mom and dad praised Alaska's pioneers, those who came before their own arrival in the Northland.

"A whole parade of men and women troop through my mind," Patty used to say. "They are the old-timers, sometimes loners, who neither hardship nor disappointment could destroy. They were our friends."

Then came the day when Patty was invited to join that sourdough fraternity, the Pioneers of Alaska. He, too, had paid his dues.

But Patty didn't live to know about another honor: In 1988, he was named a charter member of the National Mining Hall of Fame

Shortly before his death, Patty wrote a book about his family's four decades in Alaska, *North Country Challenge* (1969). The memories came easily as Patty reminisced about early days and a scene with rumbling glaciers and fast-running rivers.

"I knew that the land I loved would always be a part of me," he said. And it was.... ■

Master craftsman Harold Eastwood, builder of custom dog sleds, cabinets and other items of wood, trims log ends from one of his many log cabins. Harold and his wife, Vi, are pillars of the McKinley Park community. (Michael R. Speaks)

Traditional dances draw a large crowd of Yup'ik Eskimos at Tununak on Nelson Island off the Yukon-Kuskokwim delta. (Harry M. Walker)

Kate Persons

By Bill Sherwonit

Late winter and early spring are the seasons of Kate Persons' greatest content. This is when the weather, snowpack and daylight hours are most ideal for sled dog journeys through northwest Alaska.

"The whole country is open to travel," she says. "There's a tremendous feeling of freedom."

Travel is one of Persons' great passions, but perhaps even greater are her love for mushing, and the Arctic. All three mix gloriously together from the end of February through the end of April.

Work is what first lured Persons to the region in 1975. Just out of college, with a degree in biology, she got a job doing animal research at the Naval Arctic Research Laboratory in Barrow. Later she worked at Prudhoe Bay. But this daughter of America's heartland — she was born in Iowa City, Iowa — remained in northwest Alaska because of the landscape and the people.

"There's something about the mood of the Arctic that grips me," she says. "I became enchanted with the land. And I love the people. Right from the start, I felt really at home here."

Persons found Barrow's weather too severe, its winters too long. But she discovered "a perfect compromise" in Kotzebue, several hundred miles to the southwest. It was there, in 1981, that Persons got her first sled dogs.

"I wanted a means to get out and explore the country," she says. "I wanted to make long trips, longer than I could do on skis. I didn't like snow machines, so I decided to build a dog team."

Starting with two pups purchased from a Fairbanks musher, Persons soon built a team of 11 mixed-breed huskies. And in 1983, she and the dogs moved 40 miles north of Kotzebue to a newly constructed chum salmon hatchery in the Noatak River valley.

Here, finally, Persons found her perfect niche. Several years earlier, while flying south from Barrow, she had seen the Noatak Valley. "I remember thinking 'Wow, this is just the most beautiful place in the world,'" she says. "And then I end up living there."

Employed by the state as a fish culturist, Persons shares the site with one to three co-workers, depending on the season. She collects the chum salmon eggs, cares for them through the winter and releases them in the spring. As assistant manager of the hatchery, she also spends much time on maintenance of the facilities. She enjoys the job, but what makes the hatchery home are the dogs, the setting and the solitude. "I like living in a remote place," she says. "I'm not anti-social, but I can be very, very comfortable by myself."

The last few years, job-sharing has allowed Persons to devote her winters to mushing, a welcome arrangement for one of Alaska's most talented sled dog racers.

Persons became a racer in 1986 to improve her mushing skills. She'd already done a couple of long-distance trips — one from Kotzebue to Nome to see the end of the 1984 Iditarod, and another,

Kate Persons smiles after finishing the 1991 Hope sled dog race, the 1,000-mile run from Nome to Anadyr in the Russian Far East. (Frank P. Flavin)

with arctic explorer Pam Flowers, from Kotzebue to Barrow — but felt that racing would accelerate the learning process.

It did exactly that.

Persons' first race, with several dogs purchased from Iditarod champion Susan Butcher's kennel, was the Kobuk 220, a middle distance run from Kotzebue to Noorvik, Kiana, Selawik, back to Noorvik and back to Kotzebue. Just the training for that event "taught me more than all my previous mushing combined," she says.

Inspired by her team's performance in two Kobuk 220s, Persons graduated in 1988 to the Yukon Quest, a 1,000-mile race between Fairbanks and Whitehorse, Yukon Territory. Halfway into the race, besieged by a series of minor traumas, she "hated it." But, Persons adds, "I could never quit anything. I had to finish."

So finish she did. And her sixth-place showing brought rookie-of-the-year honors.

Persons moved up a notch in each of the next two Quests. And then, in 1991, she felt ready to try the 1,100-mile Iditarod, widely recognized as the world's most competitive long-distance sled dog race.

Persons has finished in the money every year she's entered, but it's not the money, or the recognition she seeks. It's the challenge of racing against the best, of trying to get the most from her dogs and herself.

"Back home," she says, "I use the Iditarod as an incentive to run the dogs, even when I might not want to. It gets me out into the country more than I might. And that's a good thing."

Since 1991, Persons has become enamored of another event, the Alaska-to-Russia Hope race, which follows a 1,000-mile course from Nome to Anadyr in the Russian Far East. She's won it twice, but competitive success is not the lure.

"I'd always dreamed of someday traveling in Russia with a dog team," she says. "This race gives me the chance to combine my love of travel and dogs, to see different cultures, meet new people. I love it so much." Her enthusiasm has spurred her to become fluent in the Russian language, and to consider eventually getting involved in some activity that involves the Russian-Alaska connection.

For now, Persons has no plans to leave her job, or her Noatak home. If and when she moves, it won't be far.

"I can't imagine living anywhere but northwest Alaska," she says. "It's home more than any place I've ever lived. It's where I belong." ■

Rubber-boot rock climbing on some dramatic rock face is a common pastime for Joe Ordonez of Haines. (Michael R. Speaks)

Roger Siglin

By Roger Kaye

In March 1993, Roger Siglin stood atop a windswept knoll, straining to find some feature of the vast Old Crow Flats along the Porcupine River that would place his expedition on his wrinkled map. Three hundred miles out on an 800-mile snowmobile trip from Fort Yukon to Prudhoe Bay — taking a scenic route winding east through the Yukon Territory — the expedition encountered a blanketing whiteout. Under a heavy overcast, surface and sky merged; horizon, distance and reference were gone. Ahead, lurked veiled stretches of thin ice and overflow to cross, and steep stream banks and cliffs to avoid.

Exhilarated by the extremes of terrain and remoteness that lie ahead, by the possibility of hardship and hazard, and the certainty of exertion and challenge, Siglin took a compass bearing and led his more cautious companions north, toward the Beaufort Sea.

"Roger is an adrenalin junkie," says Dr. Richard Hatten, a Fairbanks radiologist, and now veteran of three 800-mile to 1,000-mile Siglin transarctic snow machine treks. "He thrives on covering distance and challenge, and the worse it gets, the better he likes it."

Hatten recalls times when their machines became mired in frigid river overflow. "I just dreaded it, but Roger... he's unflappable. He enjoys those disasters."

"Most miserable, most memorable." That Siglinism explains, in part, the 57-year-old's passion for snowmobiling across the Arctic, backpacking across the Brooks Range or through the Australian outback and what has propelled him to a score of 20,000-foot summits in Nepal, Bolivia, Peru and Argentina.

It's also central to his penchant for avoiding routes with trails, where things are not so wonderfully apt to go wrong. "Trails have anticipated the problems, there's less unknown," he says. "Going cross-country keeps you looking farther ahead."

"You never remember the easy trips, when everything goes right," he adds.

Yet, if you can persuade Siglin to recount a few adventures, you'll realize that it's not memories of conquests or difficult destinations that are his siren's call. Nor is immersion in remote wilderness — which he dearly loves — his strongest beckoning. It has more to do with the wholly absorbing state of mind and body he experiences, something like the feeling marathon runners encounter. His travel becomes a unified flowing from one moment to the next; he's encompassed by the journey.

"That extended physical and mental exertion makes me feel good," he says. "Your concerns become basic, being warm and dry, finding rest, avoiding dangerous circumstances. Each day the rest of the world fades a little more. I need that."

Of average build and rather laconic (a master of understatement, friends say), little about Siglin suggests the tough and adventuring spirit that emerged in

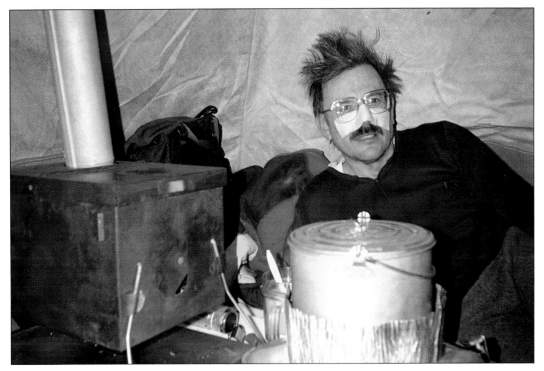

middle age. Childhood on a small Iowa farm didn't predict it. "I was a 90-pound weakling in school," he admits, "one of the skinniest in my class and unsure of my abilities."

He went to college, where an early love of hunting led to a master's degree in wildlife management, then a position as a research biologist in Illinois.

A coffee-table book on parks led Siglin, in 1966, into a fast-track career with the National Park Service. As he advanced with assignments at Big Bend, Yosemite and Yellowstone, increasing responsibility brought rising frustration with the bureaucracy. Perhaps it's no coincidence that his trips got longer and more arduous, and the itch for Alaska grew

stronger. In 1987 he became superintendent of one of the nation's preeminent wilderness parks, Gates of the Arctic. But in 1993, Siglin called it quits.

"Oh, Geez. I just survived that administrative crap," he groans. "All the unproductive time just keeping the wheels of bureaucracy going around."

The vexing frustrations were the compromises "between the right things in an ideal world and what you have to do."

"I came to Alaska with the goal of preserving the wilderness of a perfect park," he says. "But the legislation and politics don't allow it."

"The trips," he says, "let me forget about those things."

The trips, however, are not without

some internal strife. Take for instance a question that often haunts Siglin on his snow machine treks: "Is it legitimate to travel through the wilderness on a machine?"

"A big part of me," he answers, "says it is not."

What offends, besides the violate notion of machines in the wilderness, is the sign they leave. Siglin stands at the far end of the leave-no-trace camping ethic. He leaves nothing behind, except, regrettably, a machine-made trail. And worse, the snow machine knocks down some willows. That leaves a nagging concern for the experience of non-mechanized recreationists that might follow. "I'd hate to impact the purity... to take away the sense that they were there first."

Risk is also inherent in Siglin's avocation; part of the allure lies in knowing that decisions have consequences, and they can be sharp and certain. He accepts that. So does his wife, Jackie.

"It's just inside him, he can't help it," she says. "I try to ignore it."

She knows he doesn't tell her about the close calls. "But I know he's not hell-bent," she says. "His risks are calculated. He prepares thoroughly." She notes that when not on a trip, he's planning one. Evenings at home find him reading about destinations, poring over maps, working out contingencies.

Roger Siglin (left) and Paul Allen carry firewood from the Old Crow Flats area on their journey north through the Brooks Range to Prudhoe Bay. (Dick Hatten)

While conceding that in spite of meticulous preparation, he might someday run out of luck, Siglin asks, "At age 57, what percent of men are at risk because of their life habits, smoking, poor diet, lack of exercise?"

Since his recent retirement and between trips, Siglin is doing some wilderness advocacy and working against proliferation of roads across Alaska. He recently returned from a month of hiking through Australia and a climbing expedition in Bolivia where he almost made the 21,000-foot summit of Mount Sajama. He's preparing for a 1,000-mile snow machine trip to Nome and has an appointment with Denali's summit after that.

But what will he do when the years finally begin to reel him in? "I'll always be going somewhere, even if I have to hobble along with a cane, with every step a pain."

"The distance may be short," he says, "but the challenge...that will be the same." ∎

Bill Stevens
Alaska Skipper

By Peter C. Fitzmaurice

Editor's note: *Peter is chief ranger at Kenai Fjords National Park.*

The Cessna 180 taxied to the far end of the ice pan, turned and paused for a moment of optimistic anticipation. The engine roared, propeller flailed at the subzero air and the tiny craft lurched forward. Skis slipped faster and faster over the sticky snow as the three men inside willed the heavily laden bird into the air. Free of the ice pan, engine whining as if to explode, the plane barely cleared the first ice pressure ridge and bore down on a second. The fuselage cleared the icy hurdle but the landing gear did not. With a horrific jolt and rending of metal, the wheels and struts tore away. The stricken plane, engine still screaming, careened across the next pan on its newly exposed belly. In an instant, the plane skidded to a stop, the engine quit, its prop cork-screwed, and smoke poured out of the cowling and into the

frigid twilight. The three large men on board later claimed to have piled out of the door side-by-side. The plane did not burn, but clearly would never fly again. The temperature was sliding down to minus 30 degrees. They were hundreds of miles out on the Chukchi Sea pack ice, somewhere in Russian territory, and no one knew they were there. Polar bear hunters usually traveled with two planes, and several hundred yards across the ice sat their other plane, a crippled Piper Super Cub, part of its landing gear also amputated during a rough landing.

So went another day of polar bear hunting in the late 1960s. This was the Alaska Bill Stevens had dreamed about, but this predicament was clearly not part of that dream.

Like many young men and women before him, Bill Stevens came to Alaska with solid working skills, a suitcase full of dreams and little else. He also yearned for a sense of space and freedom. Alaska

was a vision, a state of mind, a place to be more than just another face in the crowd.

Born William B. Stevens in Middletown, Conn., in 1933, Bill's parents divorced when he was young, and he was sent to live with a guardian on a cattle ranch in northeastern Wyoming. At age 16, when he moved out to Tucson to join his father, the Army tried to draft him into what was becoming the Korean conflict. For reasons that remain somewhat vague to him, but perhaps are related to his own stubborn sense of self, Bill instead joined the Marines. He went to Korea as a forward observer for mortars, First Marine Division. With the end of hostilities in 1953, Bill returned to Escondido and extended his Marine tour to be a trainer. After "exactly four years and 28 days," he left the Corps. He worked for an avocado company, and then as a patrolman for the Escondido Police Department. Bill was making good money with lots of overtime, but did not see a future in this. He wanted more out of life. Somewhere along the way, the idea of Alaska was planted in his head. He nurtured that seed by subscribing to the *Fairbanks Daily News-Miner* for about a year. In spring 1956, he headed north.

In Fairbanks, Bill found a job as a bartender at the Boatel, a former riverboat that had been turned into a hotel, restaurant and bar. In its earlier days, the vessel had been a hospital ship for the Alaska Native Health Service.

Bill later found a job in the heavy maintenance shop of the Army's Fort Wainwright. He joined the Aero Club there and learned to fly.

Looking northward, Bill went to work for Wien Air Alaska and ran their lodge and business in Bettles on the Koyukuk River. He also operated Wien's small station servicing a copper mine at Dahl Creek near Kobuk in the Kobuk River valley of northwestern Alaska. The mine, with a shaft more than 1,100 feet deep, was exposing a rich lode, but the ore could only by barged out during the few ice-free months of the arctic summer and the operation eventually was abandoned.

In spring 1967, Bill landed in Kotzebue, working for Wien as their station manager. He eventually quit Wien but decided he wanted to stay in Kotzebue. Doing anything he could to earn a living, he worked on planes, loaded planes and did some flying of cargo. He joined the Police Department and

Skipper Bill Stevens swabs the deck of the M.V. Serac as it enters Resurrection Bay for the first time. The vessel's homeport is Seward. (Peter Fitzmaurice)

became the chief because it was a one-person department for a town of 2,500.

Bill also hunted a lot while living in Kotzebue. He hunted polar bears — still legal until passage of the Marine Mammal Protection Act in 1972 — and flew cover for polar bear hunters. The hunters worked from pairs of planes, flying over thousands of square miles of pack ice looking for bears. When a bear was sighted, one plane would land on the fickle sea ice while the other remained aloft. Much of the best hunting was on the Russian side of the Chukchi Sea. The Russians occasionally complained to the U.S. State Department, but in general the hunters violated Russian space with naive impunity.

The National Park Service's new patrol vessel, M.V. Serac, *is tied up at Bedwell, British Columbia. (Peter Fitzmaurice)*

Far out on the Chukchi ice pack, enshrouded in subzero darkness, the three men took stock of their situation. Bill Stevens and his friend Duane had come in the 180. The third man, a U.S. Air Force major, had flown the Cub. Apparently forgetting that he was not flying his jet, the major had landed "hot" and hard on the ice, breaking the Cub's support gear. Bill and Duane stripped everything out of the 180 so they could sleep in it; the major preferred sleeping in his tent. The Cub's prop was only slightly bent. The trio thought they might be able to splint the plane's gear with pieces torn from the 180. By jacking up the Cub and hammering its prop into an approximation of its true shape, they were able to run the engine to operate the single sideband radio from the 180, which they did every night.

On the third night, they heard the voice of Ed Ward from Kotzebue, but their signal was not strong enough for him to hear much more than squelch noise. He eventually determined their approximate position by playing "20 questions:" "On degrees, what degree do you think you are out of Kotzebue? I'll start at 180 degrees. I'll stop at every 10. You give me two clicks to go on, one click to stop. Now let's figure out how far you are out of Kotzebue. I'll start at 50 miles and go in 10 mile increments...."

In the early '70s, Bill moved back to

Fairbanks to work as a loadmaster for Alaska International Air (AIA), which later became MarkAir. The airline was flying cargo in lumbering C130s, and business was booming during the early days of development of the Prudhoe Bay oil fields. Work with AIA took him to Botswana, United Arab Emirates, Japan, and also to Seward, Alaska. In fall 1978, Bill left AIA and moved to Seward for good.

He again did anything he could to make a living, tended bar, operated boats, longshored. He learned to longline for black cod and halibut. He earned a commercial skipper's license and Master's license. He ran charter boats, the pilot boat that delivered coastal pilots to incoming ships, and fishing and tour boats. He filled in with long-shoring and construction work, and helped to build the massive Seward coal terminal and dock.

In April 1985, Bill was hired as a maintenance worker for the National Park Service at Kenai Fjords National Park in Seward. With his boat experience, he soon became operator of the park's 32-foot vessel the *Kenai Ranger*. The craft was top heavy and bow heavy, with a propensity for taking blue water over the top of its bulky flying bridge. Bill loved to hate the *Ranger*.

Bill ran the *Ranger* and other boats chartered by the Park Service through the darkest days of the *Exxon Valdez* oil spill. He transported crews for research, mapping and spill cleanup monitoring. In October 1989, Bill agreed to drive the 98-foot, 1944-vintage, wooden tugboat *Daring* from Seward to Dutch Harbor in the Aleutians. The vessel and crew

endured 100-knot winds and 40-foot seas, and eventually arrived at Dutch after leapfrogging from various safe harbors along the way.

Back in Kotzebue, Ed Ward eventually estimated that the three missing aviators were 280 miles northwest of Kotzebue, on a compass heading of 310 degrees. On the morning of their fifth day on the ice pack, with their instant coffee and survival rations growing thin, they saw a C-130 flying a search pattern far off to

Capt. Bill Stevens talks with Tom Sadler on the bridge of the M.V. Serac *en route to Seward. After a series of jobs, including pilot and policeman, Stevens found his way to Seward where he became the skipper of the National Park Service's patrol boat. Sadler is a representative of Modutech Marine, the boat's builder. (Peter Fitzmaurice)*

the southwest. The major activated his small military emergency locator transmitter (ELT) and the C-130 turned

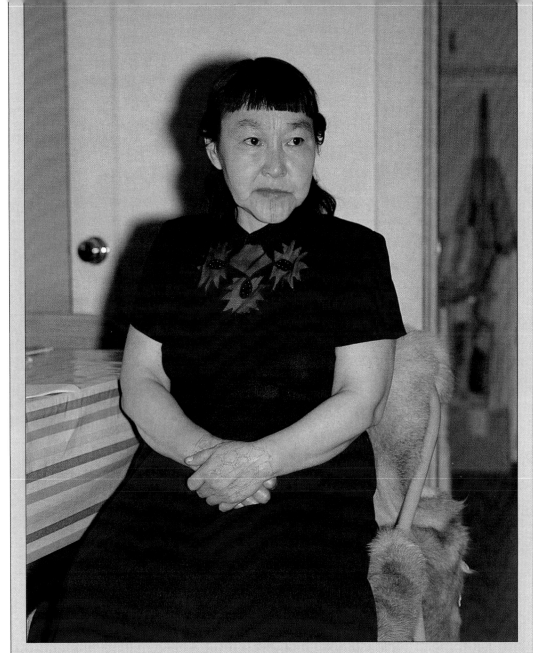

A well-known artist, Florence Malewetuk Chauncy of Gambell on St. Lawrence Island wears tattoos, a common practice in past times among her people, the Siberian Yup'ik. (Steve McCutcheon)

toward them as though pulled on a string. Soon they had three C-130s overhead at varying altitudes, but none could land on the fractured ice. Later in the day two Super Cubs out of Point Hope landed on a larger ice pan several pressure ridges away. Carrying only their rifles, the three men gingerly crawled over ice ridges and tiptoed past unseen crevasses. Behind them lay the carcasses of two airplanes and one polar bear. The major left an ELT transmitting in the Cub. They hoped to return with repair parts to fly the plane back to Kotzebue.

The crew arrived home safely, but the weather turned stormy for more than a week. Despite numerous search flights, the planes were never found. The ELT's batteries apparently failed before the weather cleared. Researchers estimate that the ice pack, a ponderous moonscape adrift in a restless sea, may move as much as 20 miles per day. Both planes most likely eventually found a home on the bottom of the Chukchi Sea.

In August 1992, Kenai Fjords National Park took delivery on a new research, support and patrol vessel. Bill is now the proud full-time operator of the 53-foot Modutech, *Serac.* In his element, the waters of Resurrection Bay and the Kenai Fjords, he is a gracious tour guide, enthusiastically sharing his knowledge and love of the area. In Seward he is respected as a highly skilled, experienced and safe vessel operator, Captain Bill. He has, after all these years, found his Alaska home in Seward. ■

Emmitt Peters

By Bill Sherwonit

On a clear and cold afternoon in early March, Ruby resident Emmitt Peters watches the frontrunners of the 1994 Iditarod Trail Sled Dog Race enter his Yukon River village. He smiles, but his heart is filled with sadness as memories of better days, glory days, flash through his head.

Known to those who follow sled dog racing as the Yukon Fox, Emmitt Peters of the Interior village of Ruby won the Iditarod Trail Sled Dog Race in 1975. The winning purse was $15,000. Peters has been a victim of the high-tech, high-cost, high-stakes atmosphere that has overtaken the Iditarod in recent years. He still races in local competitions, but without a sponsor, he can only watch as Iditarod mushers pass through Ruby every other year on the long-distance marathon to Nome. (Bill Roth, Anchorage Daily News)

Three-wheelers and four-wheelers help residents of many rural Alaskan communities get around. This group has gathered on the runway at Gambell, largest community on St. Lawrence Island. (Harry M. Walker)

It wasn't so long ago that Peters, popularly known in mushing circles as the Yukon Fox, ranked among the Iditarod's finest racers. Eleven straight years, from 1975 to 1985, he finished among the race's top 20 finishers.

Driving a team of trap line dogs, Peters won the Iditarod his rookie year in 14 days, 14 hours and 43 minutes, a speed record that lasted five years. He also took third in 1978, second in '79 and fourth in '82.

But times have changed. The Iditarod, now a high-tech race that's dominated by corporate-sponsored professional mushers who live along Alaska's road-system, has passed him by.

Peters' last two Iditarod attempts proved disheartening. Used to being a top contender, he instead dropped to also-ran status in 1990, with a 41st-place finish. "It's hard to sit and watch the big boys get away," he said with sadness.

"But I've got to face it: there's a different quality of teams now. My dogs are too big. Too slow."

The Fox intended to redeem himself in 1992, but instead met even greater disappointment. Greeted by a crowd of well-wishers that included his mother, Mary Peters, wife Edna and sons Emmitt Jr. and Emory, he reached his hometown of Ruby (646 trail miles from Anchorage) in 39th place.

With only nine dogs in harness, and several of them suffering from diarrhea, Peters decided to scratch — the first time in 13 Iditarod appearances he'd been forced to drop out of the race. It was, he admitted, the low point of his career.

Now 54, Peters says he'd like to run the Iditarod again. But only under different conditions. "I've been at the top; I know what it's like to be there, so it's hard to call it quits," he says. "But I'm not going to race with a mediocre team. The only

way to succeed nowadays is to get a sponsor. I've heard talk from people, but nothing's happened; it's so hard getting sponsors out in the villages."

Removed from the limelight, the Yukon Fox instead competes in occasional village races. If nothing else, it forces him to train his team — he still owns 20 dogs — and stay in shape. He also runs a winter trap line, catching marten, fox, lynx and wolverine. In summer, like most of his neighbors, he commercial fishes for salmon.

Whether or not Peters ever returns to Iditarod competition, mushing will remain his passion. Taught by his father Paul, who used sled dogs for trapping, freight hauling and transportation, Emmitt has been enamored of mushing since he was 6.

"People say I was born with mushing in my blood," he says. "It's always been a part of me. Always." ∎

Lena Sours

By Tricia Brown

Editor's note: *Tricia is the managing editor of* Alaska Magazine.

Lena Sours must have just finished shampooing her hair when she heard my knock. At the open door, she tilted her head and dried her wispy gray hair between the ends of a towel before she motioned for me to come inside. She said nothing.

Friends in Kotzebue had suggested I seek out this Eskimo elder, a skin-sewer renowned for the dress parkas, mukluks and mittens she had made before her eyes failed her. She was a master at sewing miniature square- and diamond-shaped pieces of hide into intricate bands of trim on the parkas' hems. The rich furs and decorative trim were symmetrically perfect, bound by tiny sinew stitches. Lena also was noted for her strict adherence to the old Eskimo ways of sewing by hand and using only natural materials, no modern shortcuts. Her works were collector's items, museum pieces.

Furthermore, I was told, Lena Sours was more than 100 years old, a survivor from a time when the Inupiat culture was unblemished by the influences of outsiders. Here was one of the last of the old tribe, and her memory was intact. She had stories to tell from an era when the city-village of Kotzebue along the shores of Kotzebue Sound off the Chukchi Sea was a Native settlement called Qikiqtaqruq. In that time, the Inupiat moved seasonally to camps where their food was most plentiful. Qikiqtaqruq was summer camp, and the site for trade fairs that drew Eskimos from all around, as far away as Siberia, for games, shared food and commerce. Lena Sours knew this place before the Europeans, before the Americans, before airplanes, grocery stores, liquor, snow machines, unemployment checks, satellites and fiber-optic cables. She had witnessed a century of change.

It was an honor to be in the presence of such a woman. As I followed her into her modest frame home, my heart was beating as if I were meeting the president.

Lena's eyes were unfocused, her vision almost gone, but she looked into my face and smiled. More than a few teeth were missing, but all the warmth was there.

"People come in, I never recognize them. I ask them who you are," she said in throaty, broken English. "But my grandchildren I know by voice all right." She walked with a rocking limp, yet with purpose. She pointed me to a dinette chair, then went into the bathroom to hang up her towel. She waddled back to the table to offer a snack of hardtack called Pilot bread, butter and jam. Moments later, she was up again, into the bedroom to find her marriage certificate — an ornate document dated Oct. 7, 1907 — to Burton O. Sours, a reindeer herder with whom she spent 58 years before his death. She still refers to him as Mr. Sours.

It wasn't long before she was back on her feet, gone to find her large-print Bible. For many years, she and her

Rye grass picked in fall and spring provides the raw materials for this basket crafted by Florence Clement, a Yup'ik Eskimo from Hooper Bay on the Yukon-Kuskokwim delta. Eskimo women choose one of two styles when making baskets, coiled or twined. Clement is crafting a coiled basket, with geometric patterns that sometimes represent symbolism from the Yup'ik culture. (Harry M. Walker)

husband were leaders in the Society of Friends (Quaker) church.

At last she sat at the table before a wall decorated with family photos, several images of Jesus Christ and a plaque that said "God is our refuge." Her right foot was crooked, the result of a long-ago break that never healed properly. "I never do make well very quick," she explained. With her legs crossed, the other foot constantly tapped the air in a beat that only she perceived. Her slippers were mismatched.

"With stick I walk around," she said. "Even without stick, I walk around. Some people come around to try to help me out. People ask me if I want to go to senior center. I say no. I like to stay with my home. Quiet place." She motioned over to the kitchen end of the open living area. "I eat from over there if I get hungry."

Lena shared the house with her youngest bachelor son, Freddie, who was out hooking for tomcod today, she said. Their home was equipped with modern appliances, running water, radio, a telephone.

Outside, it was a gray Tuesday in October. People on snow machines passed the house periodically, their engines a muffled drone. Children were still in school, last night's party-goers were still in bed.

I wanted to ask her why, how she had lived so long, but I struggled over the etiquette of such a question for several minutes. Finally, the words stumbled out. Her answer: "I take care of my body. No try to harm. I never smoke, I never drink. Nothing. Mr. Sours and I, both of us no smoke, no drinking.

"And I stay out so much in summertimes when there grow blueberries, blackberries, anytime on the tundra. All the time fresh air. That makes me maybe healthy." She paused in thought. "Maybe...I don't know." Her face dissolved into a mass of wrinkles as she laughed. "That's what I think."

Lena told me she was born on Nov. 28, 1883. She said it without hesitation, just like a 16-year-old who's applying for a driver's license. But there's no way to prove the date because no birth certificate exists. Other records conflict with what Lena says. The Society of Friends church in Kotzebue shows November 1894. Records at NANA, the regional Native corporation for the northwestern Arctic, say November 1892. And, on Nov. 28, 1982, friends and family celebrated Lena's 101st birthday. In the end, the date is almost irrelevant, an unnecessary detail in the tapestry of her story-telling.

Her talk drifted back to the sweetness, and harshness, of a life that was measured by seasons, not pages in a calendar. In her stories, wealth meant abundant meat, fish and berries. And confidence was born of an understanding of who she was within the family, the Inupiat people, the natural world.

Lena Sours was given the name "Suuyuk," after an ancestor in Point Hope, when she was born along the Noatak River at a place called Nauyauraq, between Kotzebue and Noatak. Lena was the third of four children born to Qallayauq and Ayyaiyaq, also known as William and Clara Trueblood. It was November, the time of winter camp, frozen land and bitter cold. But wood and small game were plentiful in that place, so each winter, the family came.

As the seasons changed, so did the camps. In spring, they hunted for bearded seal and beluga whales at a camp on Kotzebue Sound. Other seasons, they followed the caribou and collected berries.

"Many, many years we use a sod house. Whole family, one room. No, not like this. Whole family, one room." She lifted her arms toward the ceiling. "Have up there, window." Then she paused, her thoughts far away. "Oil lamp."

I'd seen drawings of the type of house she described, with a tunnel entrance below floor-level that trapped cold air. In the sod house, the light and heat from the seal oil lamp, and body heat, were enough to melt snow from the ceiling. No outdoor clothing was necessary.

Lena told of a day, as a girl, when she was with her mother on the tundra, and a huge black shape crossed the sky.

"We hear something noise from the air. We look around, and we see black from up that way. My mother was with them. They hollered. My mother: 'Aaaaeeeyyy! What that black one, big noise? Aaaaeeeyyy!' We didn't know it an airplane.... Big black one. Very noise.

"In wintertime, time white men and the Eskimos from Unalakleet with the dog team go to Point Hope. I saw them first time, white men."

Shortly after marriage in 1907, Burton and Lena worked in Selawik under a 10-year government contract to herd reindeer. In the years that followed, the couple again fell into the seasonal mobility that took them to their favorite places to hunt, fish and gather other Native foods from the land. And the Sours family grew. Lena bore 13 children and outlived half of them. Lena and Burton finally settled on a homestead at Kipmik, on the Noatak River. There, in 1965, Burton died.

"Nobody come around. No telephone. Too long sick up there. Pneumonia. He died. Mr. Sours died long time ago." Lena ran a hand over her face, then hooked her hair behind one ear. The pain of her loss was still with her. But, Lena said, death is nothing to be feared.

"Some Eskimo people, before they die, heard a bell ring from up there. They know. Not all of them. Then they die. That's how we know we have a real God, real Jesus, really Holy Spirit.

"I'm ready to go home to heaven. I never scared to die. No, I scared for long ago. Changes is life."

As an elder, Lena became something of a prophet to her people, calling them back to the traditional ways, to save themselves. Her words, translated from Inupiaq, rang poetic on a poster often seen around the region: "Let us tighten our bond with each other, as a knot would, and unite in love's great power to redirect the present conditions we are facing in our lives." The poster showed the brown hands of an old woman making a fishing net.

On this afternoon, Lena's own hands smoothed the pages of her Bible. Half of her left middle finger was gone, the result of an ulu accident and an infected cut.

More than a century old when she died in 1993, Inupiat Eskimo Lena Sours saw the first white people come into her homeland in the Noatak and Kobuk valleys of northwestern Alaska. (Tricia Brown)

Paul Joe hangs tomcod to dry at Nightmute on the Yukon-Kuskokwim delta. (James M. Simmen)

"No read anymore," she said. The book was open to the Psalms. I asked if she'd like me to read to her, and she said yes. The grayness of the afternoon seemed to close in around us. Time was immaterial in the presence of this old one. When she grew tired, I gathered my things and said goodbye. In the street, I realized that in all the hours of talking, she had said nothing of her own accomplishments as a seamstress, an artist.

Death came to Suuyuk on April 16, 1993. She hadn't been well for about a year, and had had to move into the small nursing wing of the Kotzebue senior center. Then the families of the elders were told that financial troubles were forcing closure. The options were either home care with paid 24-hour nursing, or transfer to the nearest city with a proper facility.

Lena had never been outside of Alaska, and had only left the northwest region once or twice for medical treatment. She told her children and grandchildren that she didn't want to be sent away, said family friend Judith Allen. "They tried to tell her they would take turns taking care of her," Allen told a newspaper reporter. "She always told them, 'I don't want to go away to die.'"

Depressed, the old woman chose to stop eating. She died within two weeks.

I read her obituary and was drawn back to that gray afternoon, her graciousness before a person wearing the skin of the people who had forever altered her world.

And I wondered if, before she died, she heard a bell ring "up there." ■

In this 1968 photo, Father Oskolkoff conducts services at the Russian Orthodox Church at Tyonek on upper Cook Inlet. (Steve McCutcheon)

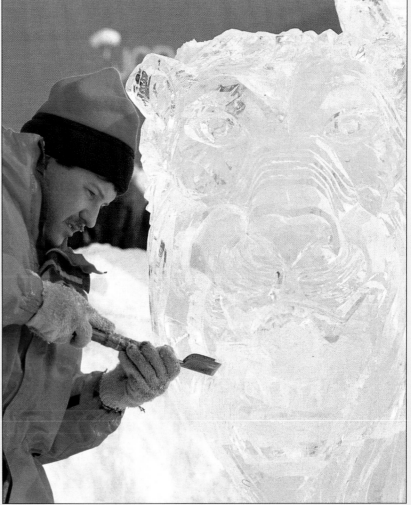

LEFT: Frank I. Reed, of a pioneer Anchorage family, and Willard Nagely, of a pioneer Talkeetna family, enjoy festivities at Anchorage's 75th anniversary celebration in 1990. (Steve McCutcheon)

ABOVE: Each winter ice-carving competitions are capturing increasing attention in Alaska. Scott Davis of Anchorage carves this bear during the International Ice Carving Festival held at the town square in Anchorage. (Harry M. Walker)

The Newsletter
ALASKA GEOGRAPHIC.

By Bill Sherwonit

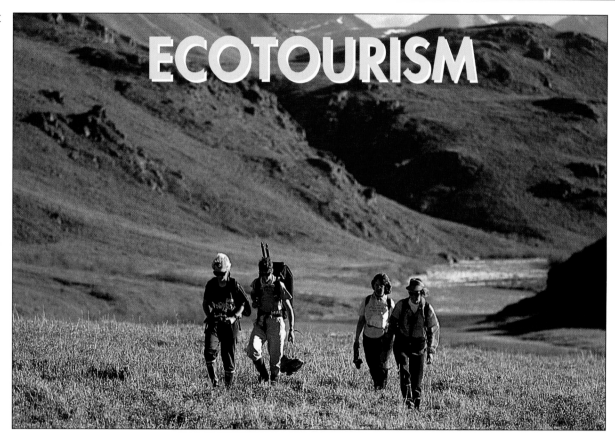

ECOTOURISM

In many areas of Alaska, hiking is the only way to reach appointed backcountry destinations. This quartet had floated the Hulahula River in the background and was hiking to a small ridge overlooking the valley in the Arctic National Wildlife Refuge. (Bill Sherwonit)

Ecotourism is booming in Alaska. From Southeast to the Arctic, hundreds of companies now run "soft adventure" tours, wildlife-viewing tours, cultural history tours and other sorts of ecotours.

Whether a traveler's interests run to whitewater rafting or ocean kayaking, wilderness lodges or archaeological digs, there's a niche for everyone who wishes to experience Alaska's wild places, wildlife and Native cultures in a respectful, low-impact manner.

The recent explosion of resource- and culture-friendly operations might, at first glance, suggest that ecotourism is a 1990s phenomenon, but that's hardly the case. The word itself may be only 4 or 5 years old, but its Alaska roots can be traced to the 1970s, if not before.

One of the first Alaskans to enter the nature tour business was Juneau's Chuck Horner, though he did so by accident. In 1972, afraid that proposed logging would ruin his favorite recreation area, Horner took Sierra Club officials and other environmental activists on a canoe trip across Admiralty Island.

Besides giving Admiralty's wilderness national attention, the canoe expedition launched a business. Inspired by calls from people who wanted to join his next trip, Horner established Alaska Discovery. From the start, he emphasized a preserve-and-protect, leave-no-trace philosophy.

Horner has since moved on to other interests, and Alaska Discovery, which touts itself as "Alaska's oldest wilderness expedition guiding company," has grown dramatically. But the company continues to follow its founder's vision.

"From the start, we've emphasized high-quality, low-impact wilderness trips," says general manager Kari Espera. "In that respect, nothing's changed in 22 years."

The competition has, however. Many ecotour-style companies now operate in Alaska Discovery's traditional Southeast playgrounds: Admiralty Island,

Glacier Bay and the Tatshenshini-Alsek rivers. But, says Espera, "we're all pretty much on friendly terms; we even coordinate schedules, and recommend other companies if we're booked."

And there are plenty of customers to share. Since 1986, the number of Alaska Discovery's clients has nearly doubled, reflecting a regionwide pattern. By some estimates, Southeast ecotourism has grown 20 to 25 percent annually since 1988.

Another company with roots in the '70s is Jim and Nancy Lethcoe's Alaska Wilderness Sailing Safaris. The Lethcoes have sailed Alaska's coastal waters for nearly a quarter century. And for the past two decades, they've taken clients on sailing cruises through Prince William Sound.

"Sailing always seemed like the best way to explore wilderness coastline; you're not dependent on fuel stops and it's low impact. We've always been concerned about our impact on wildlife and the environment," Nancy says.

The Lethcoes' earliest clients were Anchorage-area residents who wanted to learn sailing, or see Prince William Sound. Now, however, most are non-sailors from Outside, seeking a low-impact adventure with knowledgeable guides.

Although she's witnessed a steady expansion of Alaska's ecotour industry during the past decade, Nancy says "there hasn't been a sudden shift in the kind of tours people are doing; a number of us have been doing this for the past 15 to 20 years. What's shifted is our awareness. Now we better understand our dependency on healthy, sustainable natural resources, and the need to promote the conservation of those resources." She cites a prime example: As a byproduct of the *Exxon Valdez* oil-spill disaster, the Lethcoe's sailing business also was devastated. Visitors simply went elsewhere. Only recently has business approached pre-spill levels.

Recognizing the need for a unified voice, several guides and nature tour operators formed the Alaska Wilderness Recreation and Tourism Association. Born in 1991, AWRTA now boasts more than 300 members from every segment of the tourism industry; most are small, Alaska-owned operations.

"I think the membership reflects our industry's growth," says Lethcoe, a founding AWRTA member and current president. "But it's been difficult to show how much of an economic force we are because we don't have statistics. The state hasn't done any studies that separate out ecotourism."

State surveys reflect substantial visitor increases since the mid-'80s. Summer counts jumped from 497,000 in 1985 to

Specific statistics on the value of eco-tourism to Alaska's overall tourist industry are not kept, according to Nancy Lethcoe, president of the Alaska Wilderness Recreation and Tourism Association. But studies have shown that the chance to view bears in the wild is a major draw to the state. These tourists have gathered at Upper Mikfik Falls on Mikfik Creek in the famed McNeil River State Game Sanctuary. The Alaska Department of Fish and Game operates the sanctuary as a wildlife-viewing area. (Bill Sherwonit)

762,000 in 1993, a 53-percent rise. But state Division of Tourism director Mary Pignalberi admits, "We don't have any hard numbers for ecotourism. All we know is that some percentage of Alaska's visitors are doing soft adventure activities, like hiking, rafting, or wildlife watching."

Studies being done this year may shed more statistical light on ecotourism trends. But statistics aside, "There's no doubt that ecotourism is taking on a bigger role," says Pete Carlson, a development specialist in the Division of Tourism.

Interest in wildlife viewing is certainly booming. While Denali's wildlife tours continue to draw overflow crowds, a growing number of people are being lured to other parts of Alaska by birds, marine mammals and bears.

During the past decade, McNeil River's famous gathering of bears has been joined by several other viewing programs: Brooks Camp in Katmai National Park, Pack Creek on Admiralty Island, Anan Creek near Wrangell and O'Malley River on Kodiak Island. At most sites, overwhelming public interest has resulted in visitor

The Kantishna Roadhouse on the north slopes of the Alaska Range just outside Denali National Park is one of many wilderness lodges in the state that offer visitors comfort and access to outstanding scenery. (Bill Sherwonit)

restrictions to minimize impacts on bears and their habitat.

Besides agency-run programs, an increasing number of private companies now offer bear-viewing tours, most notably along the Alaska Peninsula coast.

Birders, meanwhile, are drawn in ever-bigger numbers to the Pribilofs, Aleutians, Copper River Flats, Seward Peninsula — or even the Arctic National Wildlife Refuge.

A lifelong birder who named his business Wilderness Birding Adventures, Bob Dittrick offers "high intensity, go-'til-you-drop"

trips to Nome, Dutch Harbor and Gambell on St. Lawrence Island. But he balances those springtime birding tours, usually focused along road systems, with more leisurely expeditions through remote arctic wilderness.

"The Arctic refuge is not that great from a serious birder's perspective because it has few rare species. So I get a mix of casual bird-watchers, general wildlife enthusiasts and wilderness advocates," says Dittrick, who's guided there since the mid-1980s. "The trips allow me to share my values, my

knowledge. I like turning people on to the environment."

Like most wilderness guides, Dittrick practices a low-impact ethic. His groups are small — six or seven clients, with two guides, is considered ideal — to minimize resource damage and maintain the sense of wilderness solitude. Whenever possible, he tries to avoid other parties, but that's become increasingly difficult.

"The Arctic refuge could become one of those places that's loved to death if we're not careful," Dittrick says. "There's a continuous ribbon of people down some of the popular rivers. I believe the increased use has affected the wildlife viewing. You don't get as many bears or wolves hanging out when there's lots of people."

To lessen human impacts in

Kayaks are favored transportation among ecotourists because they are quiet, leave little impact and can allow access to areas difficult to reach. This group paddles the Kenai River. (David Rhode)

tours is welcomed by AWRTA and other ecotourism advocates. "It's a worldwide trend," says Kirk Hoessle of Alaska Wildland Adventures. "People want to know more about indigenous cultures; it ties right into ecotourism's educational focus.

"Cultural tours are also a way of keeping business close to home," adds Hoessle, who helped organize Alaska's first-ever Ecotourism Workshop in 1993. "Local residents need to be economically benefited, if they're going to support tourism. It becomes an investment."

The Interior village of Huslia is one of many Native communities to now offer cultural tours. Though initially wary of any visitor programs, Huslia's 200 residents decided to actively pursue tourism in 1992. One year later, the inaugural "Athabasca Cultural Journey" attracted 18 people, mostly well-educated, affluent and from the

Lower 48. Tourists are flown in groups of six or less 250 miles from Fairbanks to Huslia, then taken by riverboat to a wilderness camp in Koyukuk National Wildlife Refuge. With an Athabaskan family as their hosts, visitors spend four days exploring the country and learning the local culture.

"What interests visitors most are the stories and traditions, the explanations of what animals and the environment mean to the Athabaskan people," says program manager Lary Schafer. "Everything is explained in a cultural context."

Cultural programs have been started at an array of Native communities, from Saxman in Southeast, to Barrow at Alaska's northernmost tip. Many, however, are linked to packaged tours more closely associated with large-scale "industrial tourism" than ecotourism.

One cultural experience that clearly fits within the ecotour genre is Afognak Native Corp.'s new "Dig Afognak" program. Travelers are invited to take a nine-day working vacation on Afognak Island, located in the Kodiak Archipelago 250 air miles from Anchorage.

Among other activities, participants in the program (officially known as "Light the Past, Spark the Future, Dig Afognak") help to excavate an abandoned Koniag Alutiiq village site, meet Afognak's Native people, learn about the culture's history and customs, and attend a traditional potlatch.

the Arctic refuge, the U.S. Fish and Wildlife Service is putting together a river-management plan; a final draft is expected late in 1994.

While wildlife-viewing and wilderness adventure have traditionally been key components of Alaska ecotravel, a new element has been recently added, Native cultural tours.

The rapid increase of cultural

The working-vacation approach has proved successful elsewhere but Dig Afognak is Alaska's first such venture. To pitch their product, program coordinators emphasize that participants "are not only helping in the timely preservation of a threatened site, but they are also supporting a tribal community as it discovers its deepest heritage."

Ecotourism's impact is further reflected by changes in Alaska's wilderness lodge industry. Across the state, more and more lodges are catering to ecotourists in search of soft adventure: kayaking, mountain biking, horseback riding, or bird-watching.

Some lodges are plush, others rustic. Most are accessible only by plane or boat, though a few can be reached by road. But all de-emphasize hunting and fishing and place a premium on helping visitors enjoy Alaska's wildness in a comfortable setting.

Typical of this new generation of eco-businesses is Harmony Point Wilderness Lodge, located near Seldovia. Built to blend with the surrounding old-growth rainforest, Harmony Point offers peace, solitude and a "gourmet-wilderness" experience.

The presence of some nearby clear-cuts "could have been an obstacle, but instead we've turned it to our advantage," says Tim Robertson, one of the lodge's co-owners. "They allow us to show people the difference between a natural, native spruce forest and the result of clear-cutting; it's an environmental lesson and people get the point very quickly."

Despite ecotourism's steady growth throughout Alaska, many of its strongest advocates express caution when considering the industry's future.

"Wilderness and wildlife are the main reasons tourists come to Alaska, so ecotourism has the potential to play an important role in the state's economy," says Nancy Lethcoe. "But the state can destroy it, too. State government — both the current administration and legislature — is anti-ecotourism; they're caught up in resource-development schemes, without considering the consequences. The future of ecotourism doesn't look good, unless attitudes change."

Similar warnings are offered by John Schoen, a state conservation biologist who's spearheaded Alaska's "Watchable Wildlife" program, an interagency project intended to enhance public opportunities for sustainable wildlife-related activities.

"Wildlife is fundamental to tourism in Alaska," Schoen says. "We're doing lots to advertise and promote wildlife-related activities, but we're investing very little in sustainable programs. If things don't change, we run the risk of killing the goose that laid our golden egg." ∎

RIGHT: Inupiat children in Kotzebue show off some of their culture's traditional skills for visitors on a cultural tour of northwestern Alaska. (Penny Rennick)

FAR RIGHT: Wildlife forms one of the cornerstones of Alaska's ecotourism industry. Pribilof Islanders have used the spectacular seabird cliffs and northern fur seal rookeries of their islands to develop a thriving ecotourism economy on their remote homeland in the Bering Sea. These tufted puffins were photographed on St. Paul Island, largest of the Pribilofs. (Bill Sherwonit)

The Alaska Game of Search and Rescue

By Chuck Thompson

Editor's note: *Born and raised in Juneau, Chuck says springer spaniels are his favorite dog.*

Sue Layton had never in her life been so glad to be licked in the face by a dog. Stranded with a broken ankle at 3,900 feet on Heintzleman Ridge near Juneau, Layton had already spent two bone-chilling nights in the wilderness with only a wet space blanket and sopping clothes for warmth. Helicopters had been combing the area since Layton had been reported late from a day hike, but had no luck in spotting the missing hiker. A bad weather front was approaching and authorities were considering calling off the search. Layton was lost, frightened and nearing the end of her endurance.

Then, miraculously, with helicopter blades still whirring around her, Layton saw a small Australian shepherd making its

A vigorous game of tug-of-war is the preferred reward during training of SEADOGS canines. Here Kirk Radich rewards Minnie, his SEADOGS candidate. (Pat Costello)

way up the narrow ledge on which she had spent the two most

terrifying nights of her life.

"All of a sudden I had this dog licking me in the face," recalls Layton with understandable emotion. "That was the first moment I knew I wasn't going to end up as a pile of bones on a mountain. I thought I was going to end up as a statistic."

After greeting Layton with a lick, the dog, Tiensing, moved quickly back down the ledge, returning moments later with her handler and owner, Marianne McNair, in tow. Both Tiensing and McNair were met with grateful hugs and Layton's ordeal was over.

Tiensing and McNair are both veterans of SEADOGS (Southeast Alaska Dogs Organized for Ground Search), the oldest and most successful canine search and rescue organization in Alaska. For 18 years, SEADOGS has been making outdoor life in the Last Frontier a little safer, participating annually in up to 40 searches involving everything from missing hunters to suicide victims. The SEADOGS' reputation for excellence is so well-known, in fact, that they were flown to Soviet Armenia in 1988 to help locate victims buried in the rubble caused by the earthquake that killed 100,000 there. They pulled similar duty in San Francisco after the 1989 Loma Prieta quake.

The man behind SEADOGS is Bruce Bowler, a 48-year-old administrator with the state who helped form the team after a Vietnam-era stint in the U.S. Air Force convinced him that the

Bruce Bowler became interested in search and rescue while training personnel for the Vietnam conflict. When he came to Alaska in 1976, he formed Southeast Alaska Dogs Organized for Ground Search, or SEADOGS. He poses here with Mayday, one of the lead dogs of the program. (Pat Costello)

search and rescue techniques he was learning and teaching were predicated as much on chance as on method.

"I was in Biloxi, Miss., training guys who were going to be called out in Vietnam to look for downed aircraft pilots," says Bowler. "The military method was to put a lot of people and a lot of vehicles in an area in a haphazard manner hoping someone would find the man. I could visualize myself being lost and not having much confidence in being found."

Following his discharge from the service, Bowler moved to Alaska in 1976 and helped organize the all-volunteer SEADOGS that same year. Other search and rescue dog groups have since been formed in Anchorage, Fairbanks, Kodiak and Sitka. He quickly learned, however, that missing person searches in Alaska could be just as tricky as those conducted in the jungles of Southeast Asia. Traditional search dog techniques, such as those employed by bloodhounds, are not feasible in Alaska where rugged terrain, heavy brush and extreme weather present unique challenges.

SEADOGS can be any of several breeds. This mature golden retriever is the retired search and rescue dog Sadie. (Pat Costello)

SEADOGS Safety Tips

By Chuck Thompson

1. *Never underestimate the danger and difficulty of Alaska's terrain.*
2. *Reliable short cuts in Alaska almost never exist. Stay on marked trails.*
3. *If you get lost, stay put. The farther you stray from your original course, the longer it will take somebody to find you.*
4. *If you get lost, make yourself visible. Aircraft are usually first out in a search and rescue operation.*
5. *Carry appropriate gear or clothing. In Alaska this usually means heavy-duty rain gear and waterproof boots.*
6. *Always leave a note or tell someone where you are going and when you expect to be back.*
7. *Keep the buddy system and don't separate from companions.*

Rescue dog Tiensing enters a snow cave during avalanche training for the SEADOGS program. (Pat Costello)

"Bloodhounds work off a scent, tracking footstep to footstep," explains Bowler, who says one search dog can cover as much territory as 30 ground searchers. "Our dogs go beyond that. In Alaska scents are maybe blown off of rocks and scattered into blueberry bushes or washed away by rain. SEADOGS track and trail scent that has blown away from the actual trail. In a search situation our dogs are running all over the place, back and forth and in circles, rather than working along a direct path. If you're not experienced with it, you might think the dogs don't know what they're doing."

"I can't say enough good about them," says Alaska State Trooper Chuck Lamica, the state's search and rescue coordinator for the Southeast region. Working in tandem with the Alaska State Troopers, which has statutory responsibility for supervising search and rescue throughout Alaska, SEADOGS have become an invaluable tool in emergency situations. "During a search in 1992, I was in a helicopter hovering within 50 feet of a missing individual and just couldn't see him through the brush. It turned out the dogs found him. There's no way we would have found him without the dogs."

Snow rescues in Alaska are even more difficult, but winter is the season when SEADOGS really out-perform all other search and rescue competition. Like their helter skelter "track and trail" method, the dogs' uncanny ability to locate and dig out avalanche victims buried under snow only seems as though it were grounded in magic. In reality, their success is the result of years of training and a keen understanding of human physiology.

"Humans have two different sets of scent glands," explains Bowler. "One works all the time and the other kicks in as a response to fear. In an avalanche, the human scent actually percolates up through the snow pack and then pools on the surface directly above the victim. The dogs find that spot and dig the victims out."

Not surprisingly, the relationship between rescue dog and handler becomes remarkably close, almost symbiotic. "The dog becomes an effective extension of the handler's five senses and the two become a team," says Bowler. "Being on call 24 hours a day means handlers have to take their dogs everywhere. Where employers allow, some of our handlers actually keep their dogs under their desk at work."

"It becomes all-consuming," says McNair, 35, who, along with Tiensing, has been involved with SEADOGS since 1989. "You're either out on searches or training. And the dogs are constantly demanding attention. They're really intense dogs."

It is that quality of intensity that Bowler looks for in SEADOGS candidates. "It's really just a hide-and-seek game to the dogs," he says. But the game has to become an obsession. Motivation is the single most critical quality a dog must possess." Indeed, a dog's typical reward for good performance during training normally consists of nothing more than a rough game of tug-of-war with an old rag. Food is discouraged as a primary method of reward.

Along with a burning desire for the game, criteria for SEADOGS canines are limited to a thick coat of fur and the stamina to search day and night in all weather and terrain conditions. The dogs are typically large enough to move easily and quickly across back-country wilderness, but small enough to fit on chair lifts and in helicopters. Breeds successfully trained as SEADOGS have included golden retrievers, German shepherds, Labrador retrievers and mixed breeds. Beyond that, it is just an instinctive knack for search and rescue that may or may not emerge, even after years of training.

"Any dog can find a person," says Bowler. "It's what happens after they're found that counts. A good search and rescue dog will recall the handler to a victim and won't leave the area until that part of the job is done."

It is those crucial "recall and refind" skills that can make the difference between life and death in Alaska where survival sometimes becomes a simple race between harsh elements and human endurance. And the grim reality is that many searches for missing persons in Alaska do not end successfully. "We've had a lot of tear jerkers," says Bowler, who acquired the lightning bolt-shaped scar over his left eye after tumbling 130 feet from a ledge during a search for a missing hunter. "We've gone on a lot of searches that didn't end like we'd liked them to."

And sometimes a successful find isn't always a pleasant find, as handler Mike Pilling found out after an especially gruesome SEADOGS initiation. Searching in Ketchikan for a suspected murder victim as part of their first official SEADOGS operation, Pilling and his dog Ruby located the man for whom they were searching...six feet under water, tied down by anchors and wrapped up in a seine net. Episodes such as these underscore the fact that search and rescue is not often a safe or seemly business.

"The dogs are trained to look for dead bodies," says McNair. "But there is so much happiness and excitement and adrenaline at the end of a successful search that it makes the whole thing worthwhile." Among the stories with happy endings is the search that brought home a group of 27 field-tripping, fourth-graders whose teacher had taken a short cut, steered the class off a marked trail and ended up lost in a confusing, marshy forest.

Sue Layton, whose story also ended on a happy note, would have to agree with McNair that the SEADOGS' heroic efforts are more than worthwhile. The Juneau resident, who turned down a free helicopter ride to the top of Heintzleman Ridge the summer following her adventure, did, in fact, turn out to be a statistic. Thanks to the SEADOGS, however, she ended up as one of the good ones.

One of the good statistics chalked up by the SEADOGS program, Sue Layton poses with her rescuer, the Australian shepherd Tiensing. (Pat Costello)

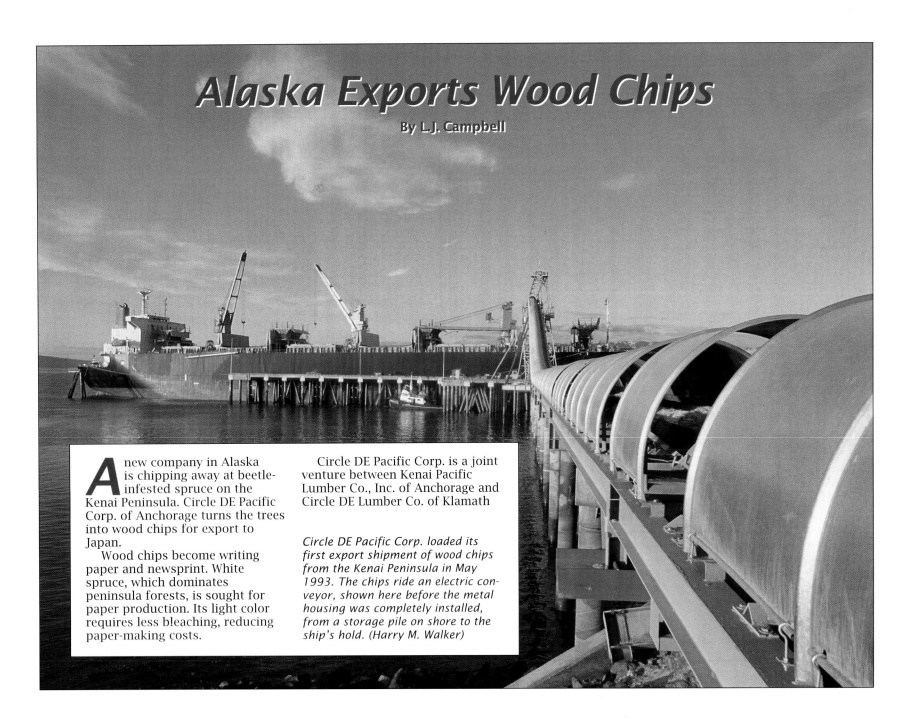

Alaska Exports Wood Chips

By L.J. Campbell

A new company in Alaska is chipping away at beetle-infested spruce on the Kenai Peninsula. Circle DE Pacific Corp. of Anchorage turns the trees into wood chips for export to Japan.

Wood chips become writing paper and newsprint. White spruce, which dominates peninsula forests, is sought for paper production. Its light color requires less bleaching, reducing paper-making costs.

Circle DE Pacific Corp. is a joint venture between Kenai Pacific Lumber Co., Inc. of Anchorage and Circle DE Lumber Co. of Klamath

Circle DE Pacific Corp. loaded its first export shipment of wood chips from the Kenai Peninsula in May 1993. The chips ride an electric conveyor, shown here before the metal housing was completely installed, from a storage pile on shore to the ship's hold. (Harry M. Walker)

Falls, Ore., a logging and wood chip operator in the Pacific Northwest.

Kenai Pacific Lumber owners Terry and Joanie Nininger saw potential in wood chips while researching alternative timber products several years ago. The Anchor River couple was cutting and exporting logs from the Kenai to Asia, a labor intensive enterprise in a roller-coaster market. Wood chips had lower, but more stable, prices with steadier export demand. They found business partners in Dan and Elouise Brown of Circle DE Lumber, who were experienced in making wood chips from Oregon's beetle-killed lodgepole pines.

Bark beetles have ravaged Alaska's spruce forests in recent years. The larvae feed on the inner bark, severing vessels that carry nutrients between the leaves and roots. Beetles have killed more than 750,000 acres of spruce trees statewide, according to a 1993 aerial survey; more than half of that acreage is on the Kenai Peninsula, said Roger Burnside, an entomologist with the state's Division of Forestry. The beetle epidemic has fueled widespread debate about forest management. Most landowners want to harvest infested timber stands before the dead trees succumb to weathering and fungi, which can decrease the wood's marketability.

In the middle of this, Circle DE found an ample supply of spruce. "We can take a beetle-infested, low-quality saw log and turn it into high-quality wood chips," said company vice president Terry Nininger. "We are generating revenue off timber that in a

Circle DE Pacific Corp. makes these wood chips from the Kenai Peninsula's beetle-killed spruce trees. A Japanese trading company exports the chips for resale to paper manufacturers. (Cliff Riedinger)

few years won't have any value."

Circle DE contracted with Cook Inlet Region Inc., a Native regional corporation, to selectively harvest 17,000 acres on the Kenai. That amounts to a six-year supply of chips, said Nininger. The company also harvests trees from two state forest tracts, from University of Alaska lands, and from the Ninilchik Native Association.

The company sells the chips to Mitsui USA, a Japanese trading company. Mitsui exports about eight shiploads for a total of 100,000 "bone dry units" of chips a year. About 25 BDUs of chips are produced from an acre of beetle-killed spruce.

The company exports the chips out of Homer, which had built a deep-water dock in 1989. It had been designed in part for a fish processing plan that never materialized, and it was getting limited use for general cargo and log shipments. The city — with about $327,000 a year in port debt payments and nearly $2

million in annual port operating and maintenance costs — was receptive to Circle DE.

The company leases five acres dockside to store its chips and pays about $260,000 a year in wharfage, said city finance director Val Koeberlein.

About 35 to 40 chip trucks travel to the port each day during peak harvest. Some residents have worried about the increased truck traffic, particularly during summer's tourist season.

An unanticipated problem arose when local kids started riding their snow boards down the mountainous chip pile. The company fenced the pile to discourage the practice. The fence helps contain the chips during high winds, although some occasionally blow into Kachemak Bay.

"For the most part I think it has been well-accepted," says Koeberlein. "It's non-polluting and the chips are biodegradable."

The chips are loaded into ships by a specially designed 1,700-foot

electric conveyor. The $3.5 million conveyor was financed by Key Bank and the state's Alaska Industrial Development and Export Authority.

Another several millions of dollars are tied up in field equipment, said Nininger. A mechanical harvester cuts the mature spruce trees at ground level and lifts them out of the stand where they are bunched and skidded to the road by the portable chipper. The bark is mechanically flailed off the trees, then the trunks and limbs are chipped. The chips are blown into 45-foot vans for delivery to Homer.

The harvest is faster and takes less manpower than traditional logging. In most cases, the understory plants and hardwoods remain relatively undisturbed, and a sprinkling of young spruce are left as seed stock.

Circle DE, with about 60 employees, is the biggest operator handling the peninsula's beetle-killed spruce. Nininger estimates the company's 1994 revenue at $12 million, up from $9 million the previous year.

Several other companies log the Kenai's beetle-infested forests for export; two of them sell cull saw logs to Circle DE for chipping. Other small companies make house shingles out of the beetle-killed spruce and use the trees in log home kits.

Becharof Fireworks Intrigue Volcanologists

By Connie M.J. Barclay

Editor's note: *Connie is a public affairs specialist with the U.S. Fish and Wildlife Service in Anchorage.*

A national wildlife refuge on the Alaska Peninsula known for its bears and caribou has attracted the keen interest of the scientific community for an unlikely natural resource treasure, its infant volcano.

In 10 days of steam, lava and fire in 1977, Ukinrek Maars — its names comes from the Yup'ik Eskimo words for "two holes in the ground" — blasted out of the tundra on what is now the Becharof National Wildlife Refuge to become among the world's youngest volcanoes. In summer 1993, some of the nation's top volcanologists converged at the volcano.

By studying the volcanoes' deposits and correlating them with events leading to its recent eruption, the scientists hoped to find the key to predicting catastrophic, explosive eruptions of volcanoes like Ukinrek Maars. One such volcano, Mount Vesuvius, became infamous for its explosive eruption that

Volcanologist Michael H. Ort studies Ukinrek Maars volcanoes within Becharof National Wildlife Refuge, 295 miles southwest of Anchorage. (Connie M.J. Barclay, U.S. Fish and Wildlife Service)

buried Pompeii in 79 A.D.

"Lots of people know about our trophy bears and caribou and great fishing on the Becharof Refuge, which was originally established as a National Wildlife Monument because of the brown bears. But most people don't realize we have anything like world-class volcanoes, too," said Ron Hood, Becharof Refuge manager. "We're pleased to be able to assist the volcanologists working out here. This place is just full of unique surprises."

Located near Becharof Lake, 295 miles southwest of Anchorage at the base of the Alaska Peninsula, Ukinrek Maars are two craters associated with nearby Mount Peulik, one of three active volcanoes on or near the refuge. One of the two craters has now filled with 150 feet of water. Maars are characterized by low volcanic cones and wide, bowl-shaped craters, and are usually formed when hot magma flows from the depths of the earth into aquifers or other water sources, causing the water to flash into steam in an explosion. They are uncommon in Alaska.

"The underlying reason for this research is to aid understanding of hydrovolcanic processes for hazards assessments," the scientists reported in their project summary. "Hydrovolcanic eruptions commonly include 'blast' events that are among the most devastating and hazardous

Southcentral Alaska has been showered with volcanic ash several times in the past few years. Ash from Augustine, Redoubt and Spurr volcanoes has disrupted air transportation and commerce throughout the region. In an effort to improve their skills at predicting volcanic eruptions, scientists have converged on Ukinrek Maars, a volcano that erupted in the 1970s with two craters, one of which is shown here. (Connie M.J. Barclay, U.S. Fish and Wildlife Service)

of all eruptions." By documenting the events that led to the Ukinrek Maars eruption, the scientists think they can help predict blast-type eruptions of similar volcanoes near populated areas, according to Michael H. Ort, a professor with Northern Arizona University and research team leader. He is assisted by researchers from the University of California, the U.S. Geological Survey and the Los Alamos National Laboratory working at the site.

In Alaska, volcanoes and wildlife seem to go together. Alaska has more national wildlife refuge land and more volcanoes than any other state. According to U.S. Geological Survey figures, Alaska has more than 80 active volcanoes, one third of the world's total. Volcanologists have documented more than 200 volcanic eruptions throughout the state.

U.S. Fish and Wildlife Service (USFWS) biologists point out that in some cases volcanoes provide

benefits for wildlife. Ron Hood has seen both caribou and bears enjoying the snowy slopes of Mount Peulik volcano, 4,835 feet high.

"I've seen bears go up there in August when its hot. They'll dig holes in the snow and climb in to cool off. Caribou go up there to get away from the insects."

USFWS biologist Ed Bailey points out that one of the largest auklet populations in the world lives on hardened lava flows on Kiska Island, part of Alaska Maritime National Wildlife Refuge. "Volcanic lava flows and landslides form cracks in crevices that provide nesting areas for puffins and auklets in

other areas on refuges as well," he said.

Since the first national wildlife refuge was established 91 years ago at Pelican Island, Fla., more than 500 refuges comprising more than 90 million acres have been designated throughout the country. Alaska's 16 national wildlife refuges, only two of which are accessible by road, encompass more than 77 million acres. These refuges support some of the world's richest wildlife resources, including several endangered species. In addition, they encompass thousands of rivers, lakes, glaciers and almost 100 volcanoes.

SHARING

Welland W. Phipps and Atlas Aviation

Recently I was browsing through your *Northwest Territories* publication, Vol. 12, No. 1, and was quite impressed. There was a lot of excellent information, plus some of the photos were wonderful. Actually, one of the photos is what inspired me to write to you.

On page 63 there was a picture of an old deHavilland Twin Otter landing on the Coppermine River. Even though I couldn't quite make out the company name on the side of the plane, the paint job looked vaguely familiar, and I was wondering if this could have been some of Atlas Aviation's old equipment?

The reason I ask is a bit complicated. Back in the '50s and early '60s, my father was a commercial pilot. Some of my earliest memories were of the tales he told of his experiences in Alaska and Arctic Canada. Dad was a hard man to impress, and as a consequence seldom remembered the names of people he'd met that long ago. But there was one name he mentioned several times, Welland W. Phipps of Atlas Aviation, at the time at Resolute, Northwest Territories.

I wonder if any further information is available on Mr. Phipps or Atlas Aviation.
—Clare Witaschek
Fairbanks, Alaska

If anyone has information to share, please send it along to ALASKA GEOGRAPHIC®, and we'll pass it to our reader. Thanks.

Shorebird Flock Flight Behavior

Editor's note: *Many of us have seen flocks of shorebirds turn sharply in flight, apparently synchronously, and wondered how the birds do this without hitting one another. This excerpt from an article paraphrased by George C. West in* Kachemak Bay Bird Watch, *No. 19, March 1994, helps explain the phenomenon. Dr. West drew upon an article by Kenneth Able in* Birding *26(1):56:1994. For more information on Kachemak Bay Bird Watch, contact Box 841, Homer, Alaska, 99603.*

The reason shorebirds do not fly into each other is that the movements of individuals within the flock are highly coordinated. Slow motion analysis of film of wheeling sandpiper flocks reveals that the majority of birds in the camera's field effected a coordinated change in flight orientation in 196 milliseconds (ms) (about two-tenths of a second). This rapid response is due to the ability of flying birds to notice and alter their flight within a very short time period. There is no consistent leader in a flock of shorebirds as any observer can see. The whole flock turns repeatedly in different directions so that different birds are leading, or at least are ahead, each time. Any individual can initiate a flock maneuver, which then spreads throughout the flock in a wave. Flock members appeared always to follow the lead of individuals banking **toward** the flock. This arbitrary rule probably helps to prevent indecision and enables the flock to respond rapidly during attacks by birds of prey.

Once one of these waves has begun, it travels through the flock at a speed that is inexplicable on the basis of what scientists know about the reaction times of birds. The propagation time of passing the maneuver on from neighbor to neighbor was about 15 ms, nearly three times faster than should be possible if flock members were simply following the action of adjacent neighbors. It appears to observers as if the birds were all turning almost at once. The rapid response is a type of chorus line effect, which means that a bird distant from the initiator of the change in flock direction can estimate or anticipate the time of arrival of the approaching maneuver, and thus respond much faster than the bird adjacent to the initiator. That bird responds in about 67 ms, much slower than subsequent members of the flock that can anticipate the coming maneuver.

Perhaps the seeming indecision of shorebird flocks that sweep back and forth wheeling and turning, trying to decide where and when to land, is because they are always reacting to the bird turning in toward the rest of the flock, which makes the whole flock veer off in a new direction. As soon as all members agree where they are heading, they can settle down to a common direction.

ALASKA GEOGRAPHIC. NEWSLETTER

Penny Rennick
EDITOR

Kathy Doogan
PRODUCTION DIRECTOR

L.J. Campbell
STAFF WRITER

Vickie Staples
CIRCULATION/DATABASE MANAGER

Pattey Parker
MARKETING MANAGER

©1994 by
The Alaska Geographic Society
P.O. Box 93370
Anchorage AK 99509

Rare Asian Shrew Found in Alaska

Finding an undetected species of mammal in the relatively simple ecosystems of subarctic North America is not something scientists usually anticipate. So it is no wonder that it came as a big surprise when Russian zoologist Nikolai Dokuchaev found a tiny Asian shrew in the mammal collection of the University of Alaska Museum in Fairbanks that was undiscovered in North America until now.

Dokuchaev was studying the 2,000 different specimens of shrews in the museum's collection when he stumbled across one tiny specimen. While all northern shrews are small and usually weigh in at a mere three grams, the specimen Dokuchaev uncovered weighed only one and a half grams.

The specimen was collected near Galena in the Yukon Valley in 1987 by Alaska Department of Fish and Game biologist Timothy Osborne. Characteristics of the jaw, when combined with tooth characteristics, ruled out the possibility of the shrew belonging to any previously discovered species in Alaska. Dokuchaev determined the shrew to be *Sorex minutissimus*, Latin for "most minute." This species of shrew had previously been known to exist only in the Russian Far East, where Dokuchaev lives and works.

According to the Russian scientist, *Sorex minutissimus* is rare even in Asia. This species now joins the substantial list of plants and animals that occur on both continents in the Bering Strait region.

—*University of Alaska Fairbanks*

K'aiiroondak: Behind the Willows,

by Richard Martin as told to Bill Pfisterer, University of Alaska Fairbanks, Center for Cross-Cultural Studies, Fairbanks, Alaska, 306 pages, 37 black and white photographs, 55 illustrations by Sandy Jamieson, 1 map, foreword and preface; soft cover, $20.

This collection of stories recalls life in Gwich'in Indian country along the Porcupine River and its tributaries. Storyteller Richard Martin, whose mother was Gwich'in, grew up here. He hunted, trapped, fished and traveled the waterways in a seminomadic lifestyle for 72 years, until his death in 1986.

Most of his 28 stories reflect a busy, transitional time in the region when trade and river commerce prospered before World War II.

The Gwich'in, who traditionally hunted migrating caribou, were increasingly settling in year-round river villages anchored by trading posts and schools. The Hudson's Bay Co. from Canada had opened a trading post and fur-buying station at Fort Yukon in 1840, in what was then Russian America. The Gwich'in trappers and families boated to Fort Yukon each June with their furs from winter trapping. This was still tradition when Martin was a boy, even though the Hudson's Bay Co. had long since moved its post up the Porcupine River and across the border to Rampart House. Martin recalls the trappers gathering outside a store in Fort Yukon, each trying to best the other with their stories. "It sound like a bunch of frogs you know."

Martin's stories depict personal experiences and historic events. He briefly talks about the men and horses of the International Boundary Commission who surveyed Alaska's border with Canada, 1910 to 1913. He tells about many of the people who lived along the river, including trader Dan Cadzow.

His stories deal with trapping, trading, building boats, using dog teams, odd visitors to the area (including a man paddling down the river on a log), Gwich'in gatherings, wrestling grizzlies, local landmarks and a traditional tale about first contact. He talks at length about starting the village of Canyon City with two other Gwich'in families, including Simon and Bella Francis. [See *ALASKA GEOGRAPHIC* Vol. 18 No. 3 for more about the Francis family.]

Martin's stories are sometimes poignant and frequently laced with humor. They also evoke drama and action. He tells a gripping account of near death from chopping his foot with an axe while trapping alone.

His ill-fated attempt to attend school in Fort Yukon at age 14 opens the book. It aptly sets the tone for the different worlds converging on the Gwich'in during that time. He sketches a series of encounters during a bewildering two-day stab at formal education that sent him trailing the mail sled back upriver to his family's home at Burnt Paw and the relative security of the wilderness. He later learned to read in the Army. A friend would read aloud to him from comic books. Then Martin would borrow and study the comic books. He relied on the Sears Roebuck catalog as his dictionary. He never learned to write.

Martin told these stories to education professor Bill Pfisterer in 1983, during a three-week boat trip up the Porcupine River. The Gwich'in title word *k'aiiroondak* means "something behind the willows." Willows are some of the first plants to reclaim cleared areas, and today willows screen abandoned sites along the river where people used to live.

Pfisterer edited *Shandaa: In My Lifetime* (1988) about the life of the late Belle Herbert of Fort Yukon. He worked 10 years on Martin's oral history, which was published in 1993. This collection also includes a story told to Martin by Myra Moses in Gwich'in and translated to English. It appears here in both languages printed side by side.

He presents the stories in poetrylike format to convey Martin's manner of speaking. This design generally works, helping the reader hear pauses, inflections and other storytelling nuances.

Pfisterer briefly introduces each story with historical background or other details that provide context. A biographical sketch about Martin is needed, however, along with an explanation of how Pfisterer met him. The map also lacks some key place names including Martin's family home of Burnt Paw. For all that we learn about Martin in this book, we are left with some basic questions.

Martin obviously knew much about the region and its people, and had a knack for storytelling. He would have been a good traveling companion. Preserved like this, his stories make good reading aloud in addition to their value as an oral history of the Porcupine River region.

—*L.J. Campbell*

Index

Bibliography

Carlson, Phyllis D. "Alaska's first census: 1880." *The Alaska Journal.* Vol. 1, No. 1: 48-53.

Cruikshank, Moses. *The Life I've Been Living.* Fairbanks: University of Alaska Press, 1986.

Goforth, J. Pennelope, editor. *Alaska Population Overview, 1991 Estimates.* Juneau: Alaska Department of Labor, 1993.

Hunt, William R. *Mountain Wilderness, Historic Resource Study For Wrangell-St. Elias National Park & Preserve.* Anchorage: National Park Service, 1991.

Rollins, Alden M., compiler. *Census Alaska: Numbers of Inhabitants, 1792-1970.* Anchorage: University of Alaska, 1978.

ALASKA GEOGRAPHIC® Holiday Gift Guide

Dear Readers:

This season, let *ALASKA GEOGRAPHIC®* do your holiday shopping for you!

The Alaska Geographic Society is pleased to offer this collection of carefully selected, high-quality merchandise, which complements any library of *ALASKA GEOGRAPHIC®* books. Society members may apply their 20% membership discount to this merchandise. And don't forget the best gift of all — a gift membership in the Alaska Geographic Society. For just $39 a year, it's the gift that keeps giving all year long!

Happy Holidays!

SPECIAL BOOK/VIDEO PACKAGES!

ALASKA GEOGRAPHIC® and Alaska Video Postcards team up to make a perfect package — now at very special package prices!

Alaska's Bears and **Alaska's Grizzlies**
Special package price: $35
Member's price: $28
(VHS or BETA;
add $10 for PAL format)

The Kenai Peninsula and **Alaska's Kenai Peninsula**
Special package price: $36
Member's price: $28.80
(VHS or BETA;
add $10 for PAL format)

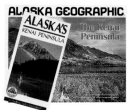

Alaska's Glaciers and **Voices from the Ice**
Special package price: $30
Member's price: $24
(VHS or BETA;
add $8 for PAL format)

SHIPPING/HANDLING:
Add $4 per set for U.S. addresses; $16 (air) or $6 (surface) per set outside U.S.

NEW!

Museum Quality Note Cards

Choose **Alaska Wildlife** or **Aurora Borealis**! Each photo has been hand-mounted on superior card stock and signed by the photographer, Tom Soucek. Each card is individually wrapped, with envelope, making these perfect for gifts, separately or as a set. Sold in sets of 6, each with a different photo (4 from each set are shown above). Specify **Wildlife** or **Aurora**.

REGULAR PRICE — $15.00 per set
MEMBER'S PRICE — $12.00 per set

SHIPPING/HANDLING: Add $2.50 per set to U.S. addresses; $5.00 (air) per set outside the U.S.

ALASKA WALL MAP

The Alaska Geographic Society and the Alaska Geographic Alliance have co-produced this beautiful, full-color 23" by 40" Alaska wall map. The map shows the whole state, with the entire Aleutian Chain in position, and features two polar views — the Northern Hemisphere and the circumpolar rim. Shipped in a tube.

REGULAR PRICE: $12.50   MEMBER'S PRICE: $10.00
SHIPPING/HANDLING: Price includes shipping to U.S. addresses; add $5.00 (air) per map outside the U.S.

Alaska Atlas and Gazetteer

If you're looking for an all-in-one collection of Alaska maps, we recommend the *Alaska Atlas and Gazetteer*. This full-color, 156-page oversized book includes topographic maps of the entire state and an index.

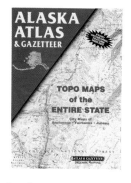

REGULAR PRICE — $22.95
MEMBER'S PRICE — $18.96

SHIPPING/HANDLING: Price includes shipping in U.S.; add $20.50 (air) or $4.00 (surface) per book outside the U.S.

ORDER FORM

NAME _____

ADDRESS _____

CITY _____

STATE/ZIP _____

DAYTIME PHONE # _____

Please send me the following items. (Attach a separate sheet if you need more space, and/or you want the items shipped to a different address. If ordering gift memberships, attach a sheet with recipient's name, address and how you'd like us to sign the gift card.)

QUANTITY	ITEM	PRICE	SHIPPING	TOTAL
Alaska Geographic® memberships ___ PERSONAL ___ GIFT	$39 US; $49 non-US	$ 0	$	
(ALL PAYMENTS IN U.S. FUNDS ONLY)		*GRAND TOTAL:*	$	

☐ **Enclosed is my check for $_____ .**

☐ **Please charge $_____ to my** ☐VISA ☐Mastercard

CARD # _____ EXP. DATE: _____

SIGNATURE _____

PRICES GOOD THROUGH MARCH 1, 1995
To order, just clip or photocopy this order form and mail it (or phone or fax credit card orders) to:

THE ALASKA GEOGRAPHIC SOCIETY
P.O. Box 93370
Anchorage, AK 99509-3370
Phone: (907) 562-0164   Fax: (907) 562-0479

ALASKA GEOGRAPHIC® Back Issues

The North Slope, Vol. 1, No. 1. Charter issue. Out of print.

One Man's Wilderness, Vol. 1, No. 2. Out of print.

Admiralty...Island in Contention, Vol. 1, No. 3. $7.50.

Fisheries of the North Pacific, Vol. 1, No. 4. Out of print.

Alaska-Yukon Wild Flowers Guide, Vol. 2, No. 1. Out of print.

Richard Harrington's Yukon, Vol. 2, No. 2. Out of print.

Prince William Sound, Vol. 2, No. 3. Out of print.

Yakutat: The Turbulent Crescent, Vol. 2, No. 4. Out of print.

Glacier Bay: Old Ice, New Land, Vol. 3, No. 1. Out of print.

The Land: Eye of the Storm, Vol. 3, No. 2. Out of print.

Richard Harrington's Antarctic, Vol. 3, No. 3. $12.95.

The Silver Years, Vol. 3, No. 4. $17.95.

Alaska's Volcanoes: Northern Link In the Ring of Fire, Vol. 4, No. 1. Out of print.

The Brooks Range, Vol. 4, No. 2. Out of print.

Kodiak: Island of Change, Vol. 4, No. 3. Out of print.

Wilderness Proposals, Vol. 4, No. 4. Out of print.

Cook Inlet Country, Vol. 5, No. 1. Out of print.

Southeast: Alaska's Panhandle, Vol. 5, No. 2. Out of print.

Bristol Bay Basin, Vol. 5, No. 3. Out of print.

Alaska Whales and Whaling, Vol. 5, No. 4. $19.95.

Yukon-Kuskokwim Delta, Vol. 6, No. 1. Out of print.

Aurora Borealis, Vol. 6, No. 2. $19.95.

Alaska's Native People, Vol. 6, No. 3. $24.95.

The Stikine River, Vol. 6, No. 4. $15.95.

Alaska's Great Interior, Vol. 7, No. 1. $17.95.

Photographic Geography of Alaska, Vol. 7, No. 2. Out of print.

The Aleutians, Vol. 7, No. 3. Out of print.

Klondike Lost, Vol. 7, No. 4. Out of print.

Wrangell-Saint Elias, Vol. 8, No. 1. $19.95.

Alaska Mammals, Vol. 8, No. 2. Out of print.

The Kotzebue Basin, Vol. 8, No. 3. $15.95.

Alaska National Interest Lands, Vol. 8, No. 4. $17.95.

Alaska's Glaciers, Vol. 9, No. 1. Revised 1993. $19.95.

Sitka and Its Ocean/Island World, Vol. 9, No. 2. Out of print.

Islands of the Seals: The Pribilofs, Vol. 9, No. 3. $15.95.

Alaska's Oil/Gas & Minerals Industry, Vol. 9, No. 4. $15.95.

Adventure Roads North, Vol. 10, No. 1. $17.95.

Anchorage and the Cook Inlet Basin, Vol. 10, No. 2. $17.95.

Alaska's Salmon Fisheries, Vol. 10, No. 3. $15.95.

Up the Koyukuk, Vol. 10, No. 4. $17.95.

Nome: City of the Golden Beaches, Vol. 11, No. 1. $15.95.

Alaska's Farms and Gardens, Vol. 11, No. 2. $15.95.

Chilkat River Valley, Vol. 11, No. 3. $15.95.

Alaska Steam, Vol. 11, No. 4. $15.95.

Northwest Territories, Vol. 12, No. 1. $17.95.

Alaska's Forest Resources, Vol. 12, No. 2. $16.95.

Alaska Native Arts and Crafts, Vol. 12, No. 3. $19.95.

Our Arctic Year, Vol. 12, No. 4. $15.95.

Where Mountains Meet the Sea: Alaska's Gulf Coast, Vol. 13, No. 1. $17.95.

Backcountry Alaska, Vol. 13, No. 2. $17.95.

British Columbia's Coast, Vol. 13, No. 3. $17.95.

Lake Clark/Lake Iliamna Country, Vol. 13, No. 4. Out of print.

Dogs of the North, Vol. 14, No. 1. $17.95.

South/Southeast Alaska, Vol. 14, No. 2. Out of print.

Alaska's Seward Peninsula, Vol. 14, No. 3. $15.95.

The Upper Yukon Basin, Vol. 14, No. 4. $17.95.

Glacier Bay: Icy Wilderness, Vol. 15, No. 1. Out of print.

Dawson City, Vol. 15, No. 2. $15.95.

Denali, Vol. 15, No. 3. $16.95. Out of print.

The Kuskokwim River, Vol. 15, No. 4. $17.95.

Katmai Country, Vol. 16, No. 1. $17.95.

North Slope Now, Vol. 16, No. 2. $15.95.

The Tanana Basin, Vol. 16, No. 3. $17.95.

The Copper Trail, Vol. 16, No. 4. $17.95.

The Nushagak Basin, Vol. 17, No. 1. $17.95.

Juneau, Vol. 17, No. 2. Out of print.

The Middle Yukon River, Vol. 17, No. 3. $17.95.

The Lower Yukon River, Vol. 17, No. 4. $17.95.

Alaska's Weather, Vol. 18, No. 1. $17.95.

Alaska's Volcanoes, Vol. 18, No. 2. $17.95.

Admiralty Island: Fortress of the Bears, Vol. 18, No. 3. $17.95.

Unalaska/Dutch Harbor, Vol. 18, No. 4. $17.95.

Skagway: A Legacy of Gold, Vol. 19, No. 1. $18.95.

ALASKA: The Great Land, Vol. 19, No. 2. $18.95.

Kodiak, Vol. 19, No. 3. $18.95.

Alaska's Railroads, Vol. 19, No. 4. $18.95.

Prince William Sound, Vol. 20, No. 1. $18.95.

Southeast Alaska, Vol. 20, No. 2. $19.95.

Arctic National Wildlife Refuge, Vol. 20, No. 3. $18.95.

Alaska's Bears, Vol. 20, No. 4. $18.95.

The Alaska Peninsula, Vol. 21, No. 1. $19.95.

The Kenai Peninsula, Vol. 21, No. 2. $19.95.

People of Alaska, Vol. 21, No. 3. $19.95.

ALL PRICES SUBJECT TO CHANGE

Your $39 membership in The Alaska Geographic Society includes four subsequent issues of *ALASKA GEOGRAPHIC*®, the Society's official quarterly. Please add $10 per year for non-U.S. memberships.

Additional membership information and free catalog are available on request. Single back issues of *ALASKA GEOGRAPHIC*® are also available. When ordering, please make payments in U.S. funds and add $2.00 postage/handling per copy for Book Rate; $4.00 per copy for Priority Mail. Inquire for non-U.S. postage rates. To order back issues send your check or money order or credit card information (including expiration date and daytime telephone number) and volumes desired to:

The Alaska Geographic Society

P.O. Box 93370-PBI
Anchorage, AK 99509-3370
Phone (907) 562-0164; Fax (907) 562-0479

NEXT ISSUE: *Prehistoric Alaska*, Vol. 21, No. 2. Alaska has its own version of Jurassic Park, only it's more aptly named Cretaceous Park. This issue will give readers an up-to-date account of Alaska's land formation, dinosaurs, prehistoric mammals and the early people who survived here before recorded history. To members 1994, with index. Price $19.95.